"*Day Job to Dream Job* is a timely solution to today's shifting employment options. Kary's proven path gives you the tools you need to launch your dream job."

—**Brian Tracy**, success expert and bestselling author

"With clear and concise insight, Kary offers a road map that guides you toward your dream. If you're one of the 86 percent unhappy with your current job, this book is the perfect place to start making changes."

—**Chris Guillebeau**, *New York Times*
bestselling author of *The $100 Startup*

"A key reason many people become stagnant is they are overwhelmed with uncertainty about where to begin making a change. Kary provides specific points of traction to help you get moving on building your dream job."

—**Todd Henry**, author of *Die Empty:
Unleash Your Best Work Every Day*

"You can help people, do what you love, and earn a great income. Kary shows us how it's possible to leave your day job and launch your dream job."

—**Scott Fay**, international speaker and bestselling
author of *Discover Your Sweet Spot*

"Many people find themselves swinging from the trapeze of life. With white knuckles we grip the bar that we think represents security. We see the other bar swing back and forth to a new platform, but we are afraid of letting go. The gap scares us and we fear falling. But what if there was a net that would make letting go a sure and safe bet? Kary provides that net in this wonderful book. Enjoy letting go and grabbing on to your dreams."

—**Paul Martinelli**, internationally acclaimed
author, speaker, trainer, and coach

"Stop punching the clock and start living your dreams! Kary tells us why 'now' is the best time to 'jailbreak' our day jobs. Even better, he shows us how to do it."

—**Dan Miller**, international speaker and bestselling
author of *48 Days to the Work You Love*

"This is it: the book you've been waiting for. *Day Job to Dream Job* is a practical guide to escaping drudgery and finding your true vocation. I highly recommend this book."

—Jeff Goi

DAY JOB to DREAM JOB

Also by Kary Oberbrunner

The Deeper Path

Your Secret Name

The Fine Line

Called

The Journey Towards Relevance

DAY JOB to DREAM JOB

PRACTICAL STEPS FOR TURNING YOUR PASSION INTO A FULL-TIME GIG

KARY OBERBRUNNER

BakerBooks

a division of Baker Publishing Group
Grand Rapids, Michigan

Published by Baker Books
a division of Baker Publishing Group
P.O. Box 6287, Grand Rapids, MI 49516-6287
www.bakerbooks.com

Printed in the United States of America

Library of Congress Cataloging-in-Publication Data
Oberbrunner, Kary, 1976–
     Day job to dream job : practical steps for turning your passion into a full-time gig / Kary Oberbrunner.
          pages cm
     Includes bibliographical references.
     ISBN 978-0-8010-1522-9 (pbk.)
     1. Career development. 2. Job satisfaction. 3. Entrepreneurship. 4. Success in business. I. Title.
     HF5381.O27 2014
     650.14—dc23   2014005620

Illustrations by Mike Rohde

Dream Job Bootcamp is a registered trademark of Kary Oberbrunner.

To protect the privacy of those who have shared their stories with the author, some details and names have been changed.

Published in association with Creative Trust Literary Group, 5141 Virginia Way, Suite 320, Brentwood, TN 37027

14 15 16 17 18 19 20   7 6 5 4 3 2 1

In keeping with biblical principles of creation stewardship, Baker Publishing Group advocates the responsible use of our natural resources. As a member of the Green Press Initiative, our company uses recycled paper when possible. The text paper of this book is composed in part of post-consumer waste.

For David Branderhorst.
My business partner and friend.
Thanks for walking with me in my transition
from day job to dream job.

And for my tribe.
If you're reading this, then chances are you're part of it.
Thanks for sharing the belief that souls were meant to be ignited.

Contents

I guess it comes down to a simple choice, really. Get busy living or get busy dying.

The Shawshank Redemption

Foreword

Some things change. And some things stay the same.

A wise person knows the difference between the two. In *Day Job to Dream Job*, it's clear my friend and colleague Kary Oberbrunner knows what's changing and what must stay the same.

The Things That Are Changing

Kary reveals how our workforce is shifting right before our eyes. Changes in retirement benefits and healthcare coverage push us faster into reimagining what's possible.

These are new realities you and I can't control.

There is, however, something you can completely control—how you'll personally respond to these inevitable changes. Kary reveals a powerful and compelling response—how NOW could be the best time to leave your day job and launch your dream job.

Instead of just telling us, he shows us how he successfully did it—even as a husband and a father of three young children.

Through a masterfully integrated metaphor from *The Shawshank Redemption*, you'll discover how you could be merely existing—locked up from your own potential. And with his nine-step "Dream Jobber

Plan," Kary gives us the key to jailbreak our jobs and turn our passion into a full-time gig.

The Things That Must Stay the Same

Kary knows certain components of good business never change. Although *Day Job to Dream Job* reveals an innovative way of approaching work and life, it still esteems proper business thought and practice.

In my book *The Fred Factor*, I share four important principles critical to discovering true success and significance:

Principle Number 1: Everyone makes a difference.

Principle Number 2: Everything is built on relationships.

Principle Number 3: You must continually create value for others, and it doesn't have to cost a penny.

Principle Number 4: You can reinvent yourself regularly.

Day Job to Dream Job recognizes these four unchanging principles and incorporates them throughout the model. Read this book, apply these nine steps, and you'll see how your own dream job is within reach.

Mark Sanborn
Award-winning speaker; bestselling author of
The Fred Factor and *You Don't Need a Title to Be a Leader*

PART 1

THE PRISON

Citizens of Shawshank

And the day came when the risk to remain tight in a bud
was more painful than the risk it took to blossom.

Anaïs Nin

So this is what freedom tastes like," I whispered.
That day the sun seemed brighter. The sky looked bigger.
The world felt warmer.

My senses of sight, sound, and smell were immediately heightened.
I knew peace, no longer hypocrisy or pretension.

Wonder and curiosity tapped me on the shoulder, two friends I
thought I'd lost somewhere along the way.

I felt free.

No stress.

No anxiety.

No fear.

Something woke me up from an uninvited slumber. I was more
aware and more alive than I ever remember feeling in my adulthood.

With one choice I exchanged captivity for creativity. Routine for risk.

At thirty-five years old I was reborn.

I escaped my day job and entered my dream job.

I knew my life would never be the same again.

I was right.

Meet the Dream Jobbers

I'm not alone. All over this world brave souls are making a bold move. The funny thing is very soon this choice may no longer seem so bold. Exchanging your day job for your dream job may soon seem like the most logical choice available. As normal as breathing air and eating food.

I call this tribe the Dream Jobbers (from here on out the DJs). I'm one of them (that story later) and I hope you become one too.

At this moment, the majority of people are seriously considering leaving their day jobs. According to a recent poll, "Eighty-six percent of the employees polled said they planned to actively look for a new position in the upcoming year. Another 8 percent said they may do so and are already networking. Only 5 percent intend to stay in their current position."[1]

This number, 86 percent, is drastically increased from just four years earlier, when only 60 percent said they planned on actively looking for a new position.[2]

What's with the increasing trend of people exchanging their day jobs for their dream jobs? For starters, the benefits are unbeatable.

Benefits of Joining the Dream Jobbers

1. **Freedom**—Go as you please.
2. **Finances**—Earn as you wish.
3. **Fulfillment**—Live as you like.

We'll take a deep dive into each of these benefits. Along the way, I'll weave in a variety of DJ stories and insert my own when appropriate. I think it will give you encouragement and perspective while planning your own day job jailbreak.

Do You Feel Trapped?

Discover Freedom—Go as You Please

About five years ago, on a Friday morning, I met my friend and builder Chet Scott at a local Panera.

"Why are you so happy?" I asked. Chet's glowing smile needed an explanation.

"Oh, nothing much," he replied with sincerity. "I guess I'm just content."

Content? Now there's a word you don't hear much, I thought.

"Tell me, Chet, why are you so content?" I joked back—sort of. Truth is, at that point in my life I *secretly* wanted to know his secret.

"Well . . . I guess I'm just at a place in life where I don't *have to* be anywhere I don't want to be," he stated.

I let his words sink in for ten seconds, then blurted out, "What planet are you living on? What do you mean you don't *have to be anywhere?*"

Despite my tone, I knew exactly what he meant. Chet spoke authentically of a freedom few people ever find. Six years prior, he'd left his day job and entered his dream job. Since then he had created a life of freedom. He only worked with his "ideal" clients and he had the bandwidth to read, write, and exercise.

His life seemed . . . light. Not easy, but light.

Me, on the other hand? I lived on a different planet. Maybe even in a different solar system. Before I made my dream job switch, a large portion of my life seemed like one big HAVE TO.

Our weekly "marathon meetings" were the worst. My coworkers and I spent nearly our whole day in one epically bad meeting. Ever hear of Patrick Lencioni's book *Death by Meeting*? His subtitle captures the conundrum: *A Leadership Fable about Solving the Most Painful Problem in Business.*

But unfortunately, at my workplace our weekly experience wasn't a fable. Come to think of it, Patrick must have placed hidden cameras in our offices to get inspiration for his book.

Maybe you've experienced these epically bad meetings at your day job too. Here are a few descriptors that might jog your memory.

Ten Components of Epically Bad Day Job Meetings

1. **Unclear Edges**—Waltz in or out when you want; we'll be here.

2. **Leaderless**—Only a ship needs a captain. Meetings are led by consensus.

3. **No Agenda**—Who needs one? This would require advance thinking.

4. **Amnesia**—Didn't we talk about that last meeting? No notes = no memory.

5. **Disengagement**—Distraction helps ease the chronic pain.

6. **Side Conversations**—You're more interesting than the perceived "agenda."

7. **No Outcome**—Let's meet to relate, not to achieve our vision or mission.

8. **Indecision**—Loops should never be closed. Let's table it until next time.

9. **No Accountability**—Nobody assigned? Nobody acts. Nobody to blame!

10. **Foggy Future**—Next meeting time and place? Not now, but only after seventeen back-and-forth emails.

Rather than forward progress, day jobs with regular meetings like this are defined by sideways energy and tons of it.

Yet all over the world, people are solving the sideways energy pandemic with one simple strategy—escaping prison by exchanging their day jobs for their dream jobs. As a result, these DJs reclaim the rights over their lives by changing the rules of the game.

These Rules Were Meant to Be Broken

Check out these rules below. Which ones do you want to follow?

Day Job Rules	Dream Job Rules
Sit in an office	Go where you want
Work 9 to 5	Work when you want
Look busy	Be productive
Expect a set pay	Set your own pay
Put off retirement	Take mini-retirements now
Boss = other people/things	You're the CEO of YOU

Although we're early in our conversation, I know what you might be thinking *even now*:

Sounds impossible.

I can't do that.

How?

If you feel like pushing back, I understand. But just like when you learned how to ride a bike, you need to suspend the judgment of knowing how. Remember back all those years? You reached a point where you had a big enough *why*.

Maybe you were sick of riding with training wheels.

Maybe you were tired of being made fun of.

Maybe you wanted to be like the older kids.

Regardless of your rationale, your *why* for riding a bike quickly turned into figuring out *how*.

Be encouraged. We'll spend the first part of the book discovering the *why*. Then the rest of the book we'll explore the *how*. I'll give you The Dream Jobber Plan, the same nine steps I've used to help hundreds of people realize their dream jobs.

You might think DJs are superhuman—or at the minimum superstars. But they're not. They're just like you and me. DJs heard the same statistics you've heard for years. The only difference is they did something about them.

You know the numbers. According to *ABC News*, Americans:

- Work more than anyone in the industrialized world
- Take less vacation
- Work longer days
- Retire later[1]

A closer look reveals that this "overworked-imprisoned" trend started decades prior. Author Juliet Schor, who wrote the bestselling book *The Overworked American* in 1992, concluded that "in 1990 Americans worked an average of nearly one month more per year than in 1970."[2]

As the years rolled by, this trend began to slowly and steadily shape expectations of work. Fast-forward to today, and you simply approach your work differently. Day Jobbers choose their work and try to fit their life in the remaining margins. They work to maintain a lifestyle they can't enjoy because they're trapped in their work. Other developed countries aren't much different. By and large we've adopted an "either/or" mindset when a "both/and" one exists too. Notice the subtle but significant differences.

The Day Jobber Mindset	The Dream Jobber Mindset
EITHER freedom OR finances	BOTH freedom AND finances
EITHER flexibility OR security	BOTH flexibility AND security
EITHER significance OR success	BOTH significance AND success

The mindset you choose is up to you. With the economic collapse of 2008, aka the Great Recession, the Day Jobber mindset seems less appealing and even less realistic.[3] Many people's promises of financial prosperity crumbled overnight. With it, their fiercely guarded nest eggs cracked unexpectedly.

All over the world, a new class of people is throwing away the Day Jobber mindset. Why spend decades earning enough money to eventually experience a brief season of freedom near the end of your life? Morbid, but true. *Why wait until you're almost dead before you start to live?*

DJs work *and* play. They create *and* rest. They've chosen to integrate their lives. In the words of L. P. Jacks, they're masters in the art of living.

> A master in the art of living draws no sharp distinction between his work and his play; his labor and his leisure; his mind and his body; his education and his recreation. He hardly knows which is which. He simply pursues his vision of excellence through whatever he is doing, and leaves others to determine whether he is working or playing. To himself, he always appears to be doing both.[4]

Imagine your friends and family seriously scratching their heads when they observe you. Not because of your new hairstyle (irrelevant for me as I don't have hair) but because of the way you work. You have so much fun because you love what you do and work doesn't seem like work.

Similarly, imagine your coworkers confused because you can't wait to spend time with your loved ones. You look forward to investing in these relationships because, like you, they're life-giving.

Freedom is the first benefit of joining the DJs. Because they've achieved freedom, they can now go as they please. They've exchanged their *have tos* for *want tos* and their day jobs for their dream jobs. But this freedom isn't the only benefit. DJs experience financial freedom too.

Do You Feel Enslaved?

Create Financial Options—
Earn as You Wish

I have a confession.

I'm not a crier. Some men are and I respect them for that. I, on the other hand, have probably cried fewer than five times in my adult life.

One of those times was on May 18, 2010. After serving nine years in my day job, I turned in my resignation. With a wife and three children under age five, I felt unprepared to enter the world of un-employment—hence the tears. That afternoon I found myself sitting in my director's office, emotionally informing him I couldn't accept my promotion with complete integrity.

Promotion? Yep.

You see, in my line of work, sometimes they appoint a successor prematurely. I felt honored they'd chosen me to run the future orga-nization. The catch? Succession was in the distant future, *like ten years away*. In the prime of my life, I wasn't comfortable making a long-term commitment to the organization. Besides, I had reserva-tions about the position overall.

Was it a good fit? Was it really my calling?

In my heart, I knew it wasn't. But I had few other options, or so I thought. Stepping back from the situation, I could see common sense trying to lead me. My head and my heart entered a great debate:

> *This is why I went to grad school—to run organizations like this one. Why wouldn't I take it?*
>
> *Thirty-three years old with a young family isn't the time to reinvent yourself.*

I felt caught between my present day job and my potential dream job. Not a fun place to be. It kind of feels like having to vomit but you can't get it out. I believed resigning was the only honorable thing to do. (Vomiting didn't seem too honorable at the time.)

Despite taking a bold stand for integrity, I'm a little embarrassed to say I came close to begging for severance. I needed to buy time to figure out how to launch my dream. At that point in my life, I had an incredibly ignorant view of finances. I didn't understand my value in the marketplace or the power of passive income—two common and fatal mistakes of many Day Jobbers.

Clearly I wasn't ready to jump.

And yet life found pleasure in pushing me dangerously close to the edge. Thankfully, I had a gracious boss and an understanding director who allowed me to keep serving on staff despite refusing the promotion. I stayed in my day job another two years, giving the organization my best efforts. I truly loved the people I served. But at the same time, I knew my day job wasn't my final destination.

In those subsequent two years I increased my awareness. I also accumulated massive clarity around how to increase personal value in the marketplace and create passive income. I'll share these discoveries, beginning with Facebook.

Meet the Facebook Photographer

You probably don't recognize the extent of your own talent. Instead, you're dependent upon external forces (like day jobs) to establish and authenticate your value. Day jobs seduce us with titles. Positions quiet our internal unrest. But as long as we work for other people's dreams we don't have to answer questions such as:

Do I truly have value in the marketplace?

If I didn't have my day job, would anyone still pay me?

If I started my dream job and someone refused to pay what I'm really worth, would I walk?

These big boy and big girl questions scare most of us away from seriously considering our dream jobs. And as long as you're comfortable with the familiar, you'll continue to play safe and small in your day job.

This was *almost* true for Julie. A brilliant photographer, for too long she considered photography only a part-time passion. Although unwilling to admit it, she secretly fantasized about one day being paid for her talent. Despite her desire, she didn't want to put herself out there and risk rejection. Eventually, a friend of a friend contacted her through Facebook.

My friend told me you're pretty good at taking photographs.

We can't pay you much, but we have a few hundred dollars budgeted.

Can you snap a few pictures of us at our wedding?

Evidently, a professional photographer's price had tipped their scales and so they messaged Julie instead.

Like a giddy little girl, she thought aloud, "A few hundred dollars? Someone's going to actually pay me to do what I love?"

In a matter of moments she messaged back, attempting to shroud her enthusiasm with a little bit of professionalism.

Thanks for your inquiry.

I think I could make something work for that budget.

Let's chat.

To the bride's surprise and delight, Julie did much more than snap a few pictures. She overdelivered and captured the couple with a unique blend of creativity and authenticity. She exceeded their expectations and word got out—and Julie has since then raised her rates. Still priced well below the industry standard, Julie is beginning to learn what her clients already know.

She's worth it.

Julie needed a little nudge, that's all. Short on self-belief, she found that a simple Facebook message acknowledging her talent pushed her over her insecurities.

Julie's self-limiting beliefs are more common than you'd think. The bulk of us grow up conditioned to see a large chasm between what we love to do and what we get paid to do. We talk ourselves into believing our passions will always be unpaid labors of love.

For the small minority who break through these self-limiting beliefs and receive funds for our products and services, we often undercharge. We'll fantasize about receiving a windfall through a hidden treasure, a lucky ticket, or an unexpected inheritance. But such income is for the most part undeserved.

Raising your rates as a result of intentionally increasing your value is much different. This type of modification flows from deeper issues. To put it frankly, most of us are uncomfortable with this type of internal exploration.

Raising your rates requires slaying some fairly big mental giants. These giants will try to scare you right back into your day job.

Raising Your Rates Means Slaying These Giants

1. **Rejection**—Dismissing your price doesn't mean they're dismissing you.
2. **Justification**—The need to prove your value puts you on the defensive.
3. **People-Pleasing**—You can't work with every client, nor should you.
4. **Discounting**—Why do the same amount of work for less pay?
5. **Cheapness**—High-maintenance clients reveal themselves at the point of sale.
6. **Ignorance**—Clients are paying for your complete journey toward greatness.

7. **Misunderstanding**—Your rates reflect equipment, insurance, education, etc.

8. **Haters**—Unhealthy people exist and you're bound to encounter some.

9. **Criticism**—Not everyone values expertise. Who cares?

10. **Lies**—Don't stoop down to the negative self-talk inside your head.

Which giants take up your headspace? How long have they lived there?

Your pricing says way more about your self-image than your personal value. Of course, some professionals overcharge their clients, but most of us do the complete opposite. If your fees are too low, it's very possible your self-image is too low.

But simply slaying mental giants isn't enough. To enter your dream job you need a new perspective on income too.

Active Income Is Limited

That May afternoon, sitting in my director's office, I only understood active income. You do the work and you get paid—*once*. When you want to get paid again, you need to spend more time, effort, and energy because the income is nonrecurring.

Obviously, active income fails to factor scalability. Since you exchange your time for a singular payment, limitations exist. Your service is limited to you—your presence, your focus, and your schedule.

In 2010, my day job represented 100 percent active income—hence the tears. I knew if I didn't work, I wouldn't make money.

Today, in my dream job, active income reflects about 50 percent of my business. This comes from my coaching, public speaking, live events, consulting, and writing.

Passive Income Is Unlimited

Passive income is different. In this structure customers and clients pay you repeatedly for work you only did once. This income is recurring because it's not limited to your presence, your focus, or your schedule.

Obviously, passive income factors scalability. You can serve five orders just as simply as five thousand. Although your product or service initially takes time to create, you'll repeatedly get paid for the original time, effort, and energy you invested.

Back then my day job represented 0 percent passive income. However, today in my dream job, passive income reflects about 50 percent of my business. This comes from my international certification programs, online products, affiliate commissions, book royalties, and audio/video recordings of my speaking.

Passive income is superior because it scales. It knows few limits because it's not finite like you. Passive income works even when you don't.

My friend Scott Fay knows this firsthand. Reflecting on his former coin-operated businesses from twenty years ago, he shared his perspective. "Something shifted inside me when I started my first passive income generated business. I enjoyed the feeling that I got to play with my kids, while my coin-operated machines were hard at work all around the city making money. This allowed me the time to do what I wanted to do."

Scott realized more time *and* more money is a win-win. I'd argue additional time is *even more* valuable than additional money. You can always gain more money. But once time passes, it's gone forever.

Your Secret Name Shocked Us

I'll never forget when my friend (now business partner) David Branderhorst and I experienced our first taste of passive income—almost by accident. Without too much thought, we created our first online program—the Your Secret Name Team.

We centered the experience around two concepts—a passive income business and a passive impact business. Notice the difference:

- Passive Income Business = INCOME from a venture in which an individual does not directly participate.[1]
- Passive Impact Business = IMPACT from a venture in which an individual does not directly participate.

Here's how it all happened. My fourth book released in September 2010. In a matter of weeks we realized this book was special without much of our own doing. The book touched on an issue common to many adults and teens alike—identity. I blended my story of overcoming self-injury with the reader's journey of discovering who they were created to be.

My friend Gabe created an interactive website that combined free tools with support from our growing community.[2] My friend Josh produced a beautiful book trailer, and we began getting emails from people of various backgrounds and struggles.[3] They told us about their newfound freedom and how they discovered a connection with their Creator, their community, and their core.[4]

Stories of victory over suicidal thoughts, depression, prostitution, workaholism, anorexia, and low self-esteem poured in. We continued sharing the message as best we could, but we'd clearly reached our capacity. My day job brought its own set of challenges and commitments. And although I entertained thoughts of jumping into my dream job full-time, book sales alone didn't come close to paying the bills.

Then it happened. I received an email from Desiree Arney, a stranger in New Jersey touched by the message. Long story short, after a couple chats David and I asked her to join our "team."

The word *team* was a bit presumptuous. Although we wanted to change the world, we didn't have a plan, a platform, or a paycheck. We figured passion was enough so we kept moving forward. A few months later we decided to have a conference and over one hundred people showed up. Toward the end of the conference we blocked off an open mic time for participants to share their thoughts about the day.

The stories of transformation people shared blew us away. Feeling momentum and divine favor, we created the Your Secret Name Team. Clearly we needed a way to multiply our impact and fund our efforts. I knew I couldn't accept every gig, and although I felt a little guilty turning down some opportunities, my family and day job took precedence.

We priced the Team at a modest $997 and in no time we added a dozen members from all over the world, including Europe and New Zealand.[5] Additional team members trickled in, and our impact and income increased slowly but steadily.

Because of our desire to alleviate suffering and pain in impoverished areas, we gifted a few slots to nonprofits in Uganda and Honduras.[6] (We felt their lack of resources shouldn't prevent them from helping those in need.)

Even better than the passive income was the passive impact.

I remember one chilly Ohio afternoon playing with my three children on the living room floor. I think Isabel won out with her game choice—sleeping giant. Our stomachs were full from a scrumptious Sunday lunch and the wood in the fireplace crackled and popped. Snowflakes fell softly outside and my wife and I smiled at each other as we tried to keep up with three active kids.

Later that evening I checked our Secret Name Facebook group. Thrilled to read the posts, I learned how that weekend three separate team members had conducted Your Secret Name events in their own cities.

I smiled. While I enjoyed my loved ones in the comfort of my home, our passive impact business was igniting. Our team was communicating this message of hope to people who needed healing. It hasn't stopped since.

Looking back, I needed to feel my fears and tears that day in May with my director. I needed to become aware of my own ignorance. Until that point, I didn't know what I didn't know.

Two years after I turned down the promotion, after extensive study and application of how to increase value in the marketplace and create passive income and impact, I finally jumped. I left my day job and pursued my dream job full-time.

Be encouraged. I'm a simple guy who's never taken a formal business class in my life. Those who know me well also know I hate numbers and calculations. When I hear terms like QuickBooks I *quickly* exit the room. Despite time in higher education, my course work was in other subjects.

I'm not unique. You'll meet many others in this book who aren't business majors either. Yet all these DJs have something fairly compelling in common—results! Despite being fearful at first, they jumped and learned how to soar.

You can too.

The Five Most Frequent Fears

If you feel a little fearful when entertaining thoughts of entering your dream job—congratulations! You're made with the same DNA as us. In my travels, I've discovered that most Day Jobbers struggle with a combination of these five fears:

Day Jobbers' Five Most Frequent Fears

1. Failure
2. Inadequate resources
3. Incompetence
4. Rejection
5. Getting stuck

Although you'll never reach a place where you eliminate fear, you must train yourself to act in spite of it. Remember, fear isn't the enemy. Inaction is.

Bestselling author Seth Godin says, "When we deny our fear, we make it stronger. Life without fear doesn't last very long—you'll be run over by a bus (or a boss) before you know it. The fearless person, on the other hand, sees the world as it is (fear included) and then makes smart (and brave) decisions."[7]

Fear, the great paralyzer, woos you to freeze, flee, or fight. This built-in response alerts you to potential danger. But remember, fear is your friend, not your enemy. Invite it. Don't fight it.

From our earliest experiences, fear helped us humans avoid extinction by guiding us into paths of self-preservation.

Times have changed. Self-preservation is no longer the goal. Who wants to reach the end of life and simply say "I made it"? Mere existence isn't your objective—deep experience is.

Don't misunderstand me, DJs feel fear too. They've just discovered how to override this internal alarm system and achieve their greater goals. They know the risks but they focus on what they'll gain rather than what they'll lose. They keep the objective front and center despite the potential dangers that lurk all around.

A story might help illustrate the point.

I detest heights, but the other day I climbed my roof. I don't usually enjoy hanging out high above the ground, but this time I had a good reason. During the past rainstorm, gallons of water flowed down our siding. My wife kindly pointed this out in case I tried to forget. Clearly our clogged gutters needed an adjustment. Good thing I had an answer.

With clean gutters the goal, I climbed the ladder with a leaf blower in hand and immediately got to work. Standing in the center of the leaf-covered roof, I looked like an expert from the old *Ghostbusters* movie—power pack and all. Those poor leaves didn't have a chance against my powerful jet stream of air. They flew off the roof and met their impending death. (Environmentalists rest easy, the leaves were *already* dead.)

In no time, I had the center of the roof clear. Still, I needed to move toward the edges to truly fix the problem. I'm not an expert at home improvement, but even I know the gutters aren't in the center. Funny thing was, the closer I got to the edge, the more shivers I felt through my legs and fingers.

Why the sudden fear?

My body fired off an internal alarm system warning me about *my impending death* only twelve inches away. Looking over the edge at a possible twenty-foot tumble persuaded me to proceed with caution. As a measure of good safety, I transitioned from my feet to my backside just to be sure. I'm sure the ghostbusters would have been impressed with my "skills."

Achieving my goal meant overriding this internal alarm system. Thankfully, those blocked gutters flowed freely in a matter of minutes. To my delight, my wife and kids acknowledged my efforts, accolades lasting all of 2.5 seconds.

While on the roof I acknowledged my fear, yet I chose to act in spite of it—something all DJs do. Fear shouldn't enslave you, it should serve you. It acts as a compass, alerting you what to do next.

Five Times You Feel Fear

In times of fear you begin to wonder, *Why exert the effort?* And why not huddle safely in the center of the "roof" of life? You can, but that's where dead people hang out. You only feel alive when you're pushed outside your comfort zones. Fear simply means, "You're in unfamiliar territory."

It visits you when you're near the edges.

Five Times You Feel Fear

1. The edges of your abilities
2. The edges of your resources
3. The edges of your understanding
4. The edges of your relationships
5. The edges of your experiences

When you push yourself beyond the edges—pay attention. In that moment you're dangerously close to a breakthrough. And that's when you're truly alive.

Author Joseph Campbell sees this as one of our highest needs. "People say that what we are seeking is a meaning for life. I don't think this is what we're really seeking. I think what we're seeking is an experience of being alive."[8]

Prepare yourself.

Critique and criticism will come for you. Every DJ encounters it. The only thing that might surprise you is the source. Most often it comes from friends and loved ones.

Their caution might come through questions:

What makes you think you can do that?

Who do you think you are?

What will you do when you fail?

Why would anyone want to hire you?

Other times their caution comes through statements:

Don't come crying back to me.

Remember, I warned you.

You'd better have a backup plan.

You don't have what it takes.

Take a deep breath. Their comments aren't meant to be painful. They're not trying to sabotage your success. They just don't want to see you get hurt.

When you don't seem fearful, loved ones often take it upon themselves to make sure you feel their fear. They'll grasp for stories, statistics, or crash-and-burn examples about your uncle who tried to do something similar and ruined his life. (Remember though, you aren't your uncle. And your dream job is different from his dream job—of creating squirt guns out of ground beef. No wonder his dream died.)

Receive their comments with gratitude. Then refocus and solidify your resolve. Many times these lectures simply reveal ignorance. They're just warnings passed on from one generation to the next.

We see this pattern clearly in the famous monkey experiment told by business professors Gary Hamel and C. K. Prahalad.

Don't Be a Squealing Monkey?

Researchers placed four monkeys in a room that had a tall pole in the center with a bunch of bananas suspended from the top.

One of the hungry monkeys started climbing the pole to get something to eat, but just as he reached out to grab a banana, he was doused with a torrent of cold water. With a squeal, the monkey abandoned its quest and retreated down the pole. Each monkey made a similar attempt, and each one was drenched with cold water. After making several attempts, they finally gave up on the irresistible bananas.

The researchers removed one of the monkeys from the room and replaced him with a new monkey. When the newcomer saw the bananas and began to climb the pole, the other three grabbed him and pulled him down to the ground. After trying to climb the pole several times and being dragged down by the others, he finally gave up and never attempted to climb the pole again.

The researchers replaced the original monkeys, one by one, with new ones, and each time a new monkey was brought in, he would be dragged down by the others before he could reach the bananas. In time, only monkeys who had never received a cold shower were in the room, but none of them would climb the pole. They prevented one another from climbing, but none of them knew why.

Much like the original monkeys, negative people try to pull you down with their criticism and critique. They've felt their own dreams within their grasp but they fell a few inches short. Rather than push through their pain, they fled instead. Now they've made it their self-appointed mission to prevent anyone else from going for their dreams.

Convinced their motives are pure, they're reminded of their failed dream every time you pursue your future dream. Uncomfortable with your action, they'll try to prevent you from feeling pain by pulling you down too.

DJs don't stoop to their level. They keep moving and growing. While others sit in scarcity and poverty, DJs soar in abundance and prosperity.

Finances are the second benefit experienced by the DJs. Because they've achieved solid finances, they earn as they wish. They've increased their value in the marketplace and their mastery of passive income. But freedom and finances aren't the only benefits. DJs experience fulfillment too.

Do You Feel Dissatisfied?

Experience Fulfillment—Live as You Like

Fulfillment comes only when you're aligned and at peace. Multitasking your day away may appear productive, but at what cost? Seems to me like stress, burnout, and depression are a high price to pay.

You might wonder, *Who isn't busy these days?* Realize this—DJs *aren't*! Here's how their pace compares with Day Jobbers:

Day Jobbers' Pace	Dream Jobbers' Pace
Undisciplined	Intentional
Focused on activity	Focused on accomplishment
Busy	Bold
Stressed	Significant
Flustered	Fulfilled

Intentional, NOT Undisciplined

DJs choose where to invest their time and therefore they multiply their impact. Day Jobbers simply add more things to their calendar. This strategy subtracts their overall impact.

Focused on Accomplishment, NOT Activity

DJs accomplish much more because they show up filled up. They contribute comprehensively, unlike Day Jobbers who are frazzled because of overactivity.

Bold, NOT Busy

DJs aren't swayed by the popular opinion of being overcommitted. They're willing to be different because they choose impact over acceptance.

Significant, NOT Stressed

Day Jobbers live from their leftovers. DJs make life their main course. DJs become significant as a natural result of their choices.

Fulfilled, NOT Flustered

DJs live as they like because they control their time. Day Jobbers have no time and therefore they have no control.

Your New Friend Named Margin

DJs naturally stand out because they prefer fulfillment over activity. This bucks against popular thinking, because most mistake relaxed for laziness and busyness for achievement.

Tim Ferriss, author of the #1 *New York Times* bestseller *The 4-Hour Workweek*, explains the fallacy of such thinking. "Being busy is a form of laziness—lazy thinking and indiscriminate action. Being overwhelmed is often as unproductive as doing nothing, and is far more unpleasant. Being selective—doing less—is the path of the productive. Focus on the important few and ignore the rest."[1]

Hmm . . . sounds sort of counterintuitive:

Do less to accomplish more.

Develop a strong core so you can be selective.

Do the best thing and cut out all the other noise.

Many Day Jobbers are still working mentally even when they're off the clock. They never turn it off or shut it down. Margins do both. They help you create space for life to catch up with you.

Have you ever tried reading something without margins? I have. Not fun. I remember back in graduate school, before the days of ebooks. For one of my classes I occasionally photocopied a few pages from a massive twenty-pound reference book. I'd shrink the text to fit the oversized page onto an 8½ by 11 piece of paper.

When my photocopies came out, I struggled trying to read the small font that ran off the edges of the page. In no time at all, my eyes would jump lines and I'd end up losing my place. Frustration would set in and the entire process proved unenjoyable at best.

This describes Day Jobbers perfectly. They keep trying to squeeze more into their schedules. Without any margins, they struggle and lose their place in life. Frustration sets in and their lives are unenjoyable at best, hardly a picture of fulfillment.

What's the solution?

If you want fulfillment, you must create something every DJ has in their life—margins!

Margins Create Space For

Laughter: You can't laugh if everything is serious.

Generosity: You can't give if you have nothing left.

Memories: You can't remember if you weren't present.

Prayer: You can't pray if you're self-sufficient.

Dreams: You can't dream if you can't imagine.

Love: You can't love if you're self-absorbed.

Exercise: You can't exercise if you don't value yourself.

Creativity: You can't create if you're merely a machine.

Experimentation: You can't experiment if you don't have time to fail.

Reflection: You can't reflect if you don't value rest.

Spontaneity: You can't be in the moment if you're stuck in the future.

Rest: You can't sit if you can't stop.

Joy: You can't pour out if you haven't been filled up.

Peace: You can't breathe deeply if you can't catch your breath.

Friendships: You can't expect to have friends if you fail to be one.

You can't survive without food, water, or sleep. (College students might disagree with the *sleep* part.) Yet many people believe you can survive *and even thrive* without margins. Your Designer seemed to think otherwise by gifting you one full day of rest and recreation in every seven.

Recreate. I love that word. It reminds me:

We're unfinished and still in process.

We're alive and growing and in need of input.

We weren't simply created to produce.

Machines, on the other hand? They're created specifically for output. We place higher value on machines with a higher capacity for output.

Humans are different. We're not machines. We're a beautiful blend of:

Body, soul, and spirit

Sex, sweat, and laughter

Tears, hopes, and longings

Desires, fears, and dreams

You need rest and recreation. These two essential components fuel fulfillment.

Human Doings or Human Beings?

When you check out of life only to produce within the prison called your "day job," something inside you dies. Busyness may mask the pain, but it certainly doesn't eliminate it.

Consider this:

- Life is too short to spend tens of thousands of hours in misery.
- Life is too short to be living in chronic pain just to survive until another weekend.
- Life is too short *not* to make the maximum contribution with the gifts and abilities entrusted to you.
- Life is too short to hold on to a job for the sole reason of a paycheck or retirement benefits.

Steve Jobs understood this brevity. It served as a filter for his choices, including his employment ones.

> When I was 17, I read a quote that went something like: "If you live each day as if it was your last, someday you'll most certainly be right." It made an impression on me, and since then, for the past 33 years, I have looked in the mirror every morning and asked myself: "If today were the last day of my life, would I want to do what I am about to do today?" And whenever the answer has been "No" for too many days in a row, I know I need to change something.[2]

Easy to say but difficult to do, right?

But consider the unique time in which you live. For thousands of years humanity was, for the most part, stuck with their fate. Choices eluded us and we were locked into our lot in life. If your daddy or grandpa was a blacksmith, then likely so were you. If you were born into an agrarian environment, then you probably stayed there.

Not so today. Regardless of what you believe, you *do* have a choice. You can live as you'd like.

Fulfillment is the third benefit of joining the DJs. Because they're fulfilled, they live as they like. They've exchanged activities for accomplishment and their day jobs for their dream jobs.

Now that you know the three benefits of the DJs (freedom, finances, and fulfillment), the better question is—When can you start?

Why the "When" Is "Now"

I t's a great time to be alive and your chances for success are far greater today than at any other time in human history. According to Darren Hardy, who cofounded an internet company in early 2000, "Your chance at entrepreneurial success is 564 times greater than just 13 years ago."[1]

He explains why.

> We raised several million dollars to get started [in 2000]. Building the website, the software to run it and servers to deliver it cost nearly $1 million. Today that website could be built for less than $5,000. We spent the other millions to hire experienced tech talent (we paid a high price because of limited supply) and on marketing in the days before Google AdWords, Facebook, Twitter, Pinterest, etc.[2]

Besides these encouraging odds, there are five additional reasons why the time is right to exchange your day job for your dream job.

Five Reasons Why the "When" Is "Now"

1. More Access ("The Who")

If you know the right rules and abide by them, no one is beyond your reach.

In 2004, Tony Blair became the first prime minister to master text messaging publicly. He used this technology to answer questions directly sent to him from his citizens.[3] Imagine what people would have thought thirty years ago about directly communicating with the leader of their country about political policies. No commoner had access like that.

Today you can communicate with government officials, professional athletes, experts, celebrities, and prominent religious leaders quite simply.

Some strategies are more effective than others and plenty of websites share their opinions on the matter. They range from connecting through paid phone calls to negotiating personal meetings.[4]

DJs connect with leaders through relational strategies—ones that give back value instead of merely taking.

Just last week I sat at a park in Powell, Ohio, framing up some chapters for this book. I found myself reading *The $100 Startup* for the third time. The humble and competent Chris Guillebeau wrote this amazing *New York Times* bestseller. This book helped me find my wings a couple years ago when I struggled about leaving my day job. I felt indebted to Chris for his wisdom and work, and I wanted to express my gratitude.

While reading his book, I also had one quick question. I thought, *If only he were in the park. Then I could ask him. Bummer.*

Rather than letting that whim pass me by, I did something else. *I took action.* I went to Chris's website and spent some time looking around. Not only did my appreciation for him soon grow but also my desire to shoot him a quick note of encouragement.

After a few minutes I found his contact info and wrote him a quick thank-you. I also included my simple question. Then I clicked *send* and quite naturally went back to reading.

Within five minutes I received a brief but personal email from Chris himself. He even answered my question with a resounding YES.

Knowing Chris's schedule, he probably got my message while traveling somewhere in Norway or India. (He's visited every country in the world between 2002 and 2013.)

Nonetheless, I found the whole exchange rather ironic. Five minutes before I found myself reading an insightful book. Fast-forward a few minutes and now I was having an email conversation with this insightful author.

My experience isn't unique.

If you know the right rules and abide by them, you can access previously "unreachable" people. It helps if the person you're trying to reach is a kind and generous human being like Chris. Nonetheless, I framed my email according to a certain set of rules.

Use the rules and you come across as informed. Abuse the rules and you come across as ignorant. The choice is up to you.

We'll unpack these rules and many other helpful strategies in The Dream Jobber Plan. For now, just remember that today you have more access to the people you need to connect with than at any other time in human history.

2. More Resources ("The What")

If you know where to go, the world is at your fingertips, literally.

In July 2008 the iPhone App Store had only eight hundred apps (application software). Five years later that number has jumped to over one million apps.[5] And that does not include all of the apps available for other smartphones (I use this disclaimer to avoid any wars with Android friends, etc.). Some apps may relate to your dream job, others may not.[6]

There is an app for writing emails while you walk, for on-the-spot payments, for remotely accessing your computer, for help with invoicing and time tracking, and many others. (For a longer description on many useful apps currently available, visit DayJobToDreamJob.com.) I only mention a few apps to illustrate a point. You have more than one million left to explore. (I'd warn against this though.)

My point?

You have more resources available than you'll ever need. You also have more allies committed to your success than ever before. Breathe easy because you're not alone.

You have chat rooms and online communities ready to serve you. People today want to help, even with the simplest of questions. You no longer need the yellow pages. (Do they still have those?) Just ask your Twitter followers for the name of a trusted mechanic or an unbeatable speed-reading course. They'll jump in and offer advice.

In past stories and folklore, heroes received gifts of special super-powers to aid them in accomplishing their mission. Lady Galadriel and

Lord Celeborn granted Elvish items to the remaining members of the Fellowship of the Ring.[7] Frodo received the Light of Eärendil, which emitted a brilliant light in the darkness to help him on his journey.

Today, you can get a free flashlight app for your smartphone to help you on your journey. (Same effect, although the name is definitely not as cool as the Elvish version.)

My advice?

Don't wait for an elf. Visit the App Store or Google Marketplace instead. Today, many of our "superpowers" come via technology, communities, and resources.

3. More Connected ("The Where")

If you can get online, you can run your businesses.

I don't need to convince you because you probably already know—physical space is no longer a barrier that keeps you from starting your dream job. Currently, I'm outside enjoying the weather on a beautiful afternoon. The only drawback? To get to my destination I had to walk through a minefield of geese droppings. Nonetheless, I'm presently overlooking a quaint pond, sitting on a soft bed of pine needles, listening to an epic soundtrack, and writing to you on my laptop.

I'm living my dream job.

Ten minutes ago, when I checked my phone, I had three messages requesting my response. One from a select coaching client. One requesting me to do a presentation on one of my books two months from now. And one request for a retreat with business leaders next spring.

I conduct all this "business" without an office. At this point in my life, I *choose* not to have an office. This might cause some people to lose respect for me.

Aren't I "big" enough to warrant an office?

What if my clients find out I don't have one?

Will my clients think less of me?

Will I lose the ability to negotiate fair fees for my services?

Am I secretly a bum?

Perhaps it sounds a little odd, but I'm not worried if my clients find out. *I've actually already told them.*

My choice isn't related to an expense issue but a lifestyle one.

I've had a beautiful office space offered to me free of charge, no strings attached. I graciously turned it down for no other reason than the fact that an office doesn't fit my business or my lifestyle.

Keep in mind, DJs design, create, and maintain structures and strategies that support their goals. A physical office doesn't support my goal of freedom. I spent more than a decade tied to my day job. In that period I had an abundant amount of *have tos*:

I *have to* go to that meeting.

I *have to* work outside my strength zone.

I *have to* miss that event.

I realized that although I was doing many "good things," the price was more than I was willing to pay. Sure I had health insurance, a steady paycheck, and an amazing community—but I didn't have my freedom.

Now I do. And because I do, I'm keenly aware of adding anything that limits my freedom. Currently, my wife and I could pick up for the next three months and travel internationally with our kids.

How?

I run my business predominantly with my laptop and my smartphone. These two tools have enabled me to do some amazing things such as:

Start a nonprofit.

Participate in masterminds with my clients and New York publishers.

Close six-figure contracts.

All this action stemmed from the convenience of coffee shop patios with WiFi connections.

As a general practice, I don't tell other people they *don't* need office space. Maybe they *do*. It might serve their lifestyle and business well.

Personally, it makes me claustrophobic. Instead of that office space serving me, in no time at all I'd be serving *it*. I'd feel the need to go "into the office" to justify having the address printed on my business card.

Many agree that *an office is where an entrepreneur goes to hide from opportunities*. And because I'm an entrepreneur, I want to be close to opportunities. I also want to be close to what I value—my wife and kids.

Besides, what kind of author, coach, and speaker lives at a desk? *Not a very good one*. John le Carré warns, "A desk is a dangerous place from which to view the world."[8]

Don't misunderstand—I'm not against offices. But I'm vehemently against the lies that hold you back from your dream job. A common one holding many back is that you need a tremendous amount of capital devoted to office space before you open up shop.

Really?

Most people who pay for their office space feel guilty if they don't use it. They feel the need to show up in their artificial environment to make their magic happen. And so, most office-space occupiers settle right back into a 9 to 5 routine because it's the model we've all witnessed for decades.

Pretty soon these folks are buying staplers, desks, chairs, wall calendars, and dry-erase boards because that's what they were told an office needs.

With high monthly overhead devoted to office supplies that fill new desks and employees that fill empty cubicles, they soon get sucked into "the crazy cycle." Beginning financially in the hole every month, they take on less than ideal clients to simply "break even." They fail to see the new prison they're designing. Fast-forward twelve months and they have a full slate of toxic clients. They wonder how they got there. They resort to dressing up like a ten-year-old so they can sell Girl Scout cookies on the weekends and earn some extra cash.

TIME OUT from this scary nightmare!

Who says you need an office?

Who says you need employees?

Who says you need to dress like a Girl Scout?

This is the new frontier. Traditional business protocols no longer control you. You're free to explore, create, and innovate.

Don't believe me?

Meet Mike Myers—not the famous comedian but the accomplished educator.[9] He has a single mission—*to magnify the talents inside his students so they can realize confidence and success.* He founded Talents Tutoring:

Without a partner

Without employees

Without office space

He began the same way all DJs do—with a dream. That dream turned into a website and then into a business. Now if a child wants immediate tutoring from Mike, good luck. He's booked solid, even after raising his rates.

For years Mike worked as a teacher during the school year and then ran a painting business during the summer. The three-month painting business eventually took its toll. No painter simply shows up in June with a full set of clients. Mike would begin bidding jobs as early as January, making it difficult to balance his teaching job and his home life.

After a little coaching, Mike decided to take the big step. He sold all his painting equipment and started his tutoring business. By following The Dream Jobber Plan, Mike transitioned into a sought-after tutor.

Since then he automated his scheduling and payment processes, which let him invest more time in his wife and new child. He created a vibrant summer business that complements his teaching profession the rest of the year.

Office space, employees, and every other perceived "prerequisite" are simply excuses to delay your dream job. Trust me—if you can get online you can run your business.

For those doubters in the house, I'm not claiming your dream job is at that place now, but it could be. Through outsourcing, freelancing, and independent contractors, your business can run incredibly lean. That is, if you want it lean.

Some don't. But we'll explore those alternatives too.

Remember, in this space all your "have tos" are now up for grabs. You're redefining the rules and creating a new life of "want tos."

4. More Incentive ("The Why")

If you don't have to stay, why would you?

There's five reasons why you should start your dream job. We'll unpack them one by one.

Five Reasons Why You Should Start Your Dream Job

1. Your day job isn't permanent.
2. Your engagement level will increase.
3. You'll become a master in the art of living.
4. People's lives will change.
5. You will live longer.

1. YOUR DAY JOB ISN'T PERMANENT

Meet John, Nancy, and Louise. Each of them used to think they had to stay in their day jobs. John had been in his company for sixteen years, Nancy for twenty, and Louise for twelve. Over the years, each built true results, solid seniority, and close friendships. John commented, "My company felt like my second family."

Without any forewarning, each were told their day jobs would be eliminated.

Nancy explained the weird twist, "For the past fifteen years my job was to help other people in the company transition out. Overnight I learned that I'd be the one transitioning."

Nancy's, John's, and Louise's credentials seemed bulletproof . . . or so they thought. Still, when the corporate axe swings, someone's head has to fall. Unfortunately, John had relocated just six months before receiving his shocking news. He soon found himself in a new town, in a new house, and unemployed.

"I couldn't believe it," John explained. "For a few weeks after the news I really doubted myself. I kept wondering what did I do wrong? But the truth is I didn't do anything wrong. My wife had to go back to work and our family roles shifted quickly."

John, Louise, and Nancy each have kids in high school or college. Each has a beautiful home and rich friendships. But despite their personal plans, their companies had other ones.

Whether you're ready to accept it or not, statistics demonstrate a brand-new world:

Unemployment—In the last five years, the unemployment rate approached 10 percent.[10]

Jobs—The Bureau of Labor Statistics (BLS) reports that people hold an average of eleven jobs just between ages 18 to 44.[11]

Careers—The average US worker will have many careers—seven is the most widely cited number—in his or her lifetime.[12]

Length—The BLS reports that the median number of years that wage and salary workers remain with their employer is 4.6 years.[13]

Roles—"Studies estimate half of the American workforce will soon consist of freelancers, consultants, independent contractors, entrepreneurs, 'electronic immigrants,' and so forth."[14]

In summary, the average worker will change her career seven times, hold eleven jobs before the age of forty-four, remain in her current place of employment for less than five years, and probably move into a freelance/independent contractor role.

Few people remain in their companies for twenty, sixteen, or even twelve years. John, Nancy, and Louise were the exception. And in each situation, the transition was done to them, not the other way around. Even if you want to believe your day job is safe, secure, and permanent, it's not.

This is why you must prepare yourself for your dream job now, not later. In the case of Nancy and Louise, providentially each was engaged in my Deeper Path Coaching Cohort *before* receiving the tough news.[15] Part of the process requires them to write out their dream job with crystal clarity.

Louise commented, "If I wasn't working on my dream before I got the news, I would've been shell-shocked. Because I'd already identified it, when I was told my job was eliminated I actually felt some relief.

In a strange way, it was the permission I needed to go out and start my dream job."

Louise has done just that. She took a course on how to manage her own website and maintain her own social media and then she launched her business. Just like that.

"I feel alive again." She chuckled. "I don't know why I waited so long. The other day, one of my clients sincerely thanked me for the value I'm providing her. She said many of her relationships are improving because of our work together. I know this is what I was created to do and I'm overflowing with gratitude."

Louise needed to be kicked out of the nest before she learned how to fly. Nancy and John are flying in their dream jobs too.

Just the other day, Nancy told me, "Through the Cohort I wrote out my purpose: *exposing students' big ideas by nourishing their dreams and guiding their intentions.* Because I now know what I really want, I just accepted a job offer at one of the largest universities in the country. I get paid to coach students as they develop and launch their careers."

Was the jump scary? Sure.

But too many times we focus on the cost of acting. DJs flip the equation. They do serious reflection on the cost of *not* acting. They take inventory of what will happen if they *stay* in their day job rather than if they *leave.*

Louise had no idea what she was missing because she was so focused on producing results. Life passed her by as she climbed the corporate ladder. Ironically, the ladder eventually broke. Looking back, she admits there were obvious gaps along the way.

"On an increasing basis my boss required me to make key decisions against my gut. I hated implementing those decisions. They bordered on unethical. At a minimum they were poor leadership decisions. I went with them because I didn't have any other options."

2. Your Engagement Level Will Increase

Louise now realizes in her last few years on the job she suffered from disengagement.

She's not that unique. The Gallup Organization regularly surveys employees in the United States and around the world. They've discovered some shocking statistics about engagement in the work-place. The most recent findings for US workers may surprise you. (Many other countries reveal an even dimmer reality.[16])

Not Engaged—52 percent of the United States working popu-lation is not engaged. These people do just enough to get a paycheck. Merely going through the motions, if they feel they could leave their day jobs they would. They live and work from half a heart.

Actively Disengaged—18 percent of the United States working population is actively disengaged. These people take calculated, strategic steps to steal from their employer, spread lies about coworkers, and create disunity in their work environment. They communicate their disengagement through unproductive ac-tions. They sabotage themselves and those around them. They're not bad people, but they're "stuck" people acting negatively. They live and work from a broken heart.

Engaged—30 percent of the United States working population is engaged. This small segment takes responsibility and ownership for their assignments. They realize their work is an extension of themselves and because they're on fire, so is everything they touch. They live and work from a full heart.[17]

Based on this Gallup research, 70 percent of US workers desire to leave their current day job. They stay because they don't think they can transition to their dream job or they struggle knowing how.

Of course, all this disengagement carries a financial cost, "up to $550 billion annually in lost productivity."[18] And in addition to the expense in dollars there's an emotional one too.

3. You'll Become a Master in the Art of Living

Swiss psychiatrist Carl Jung said, "The greatest burden a child must bear is the unlived life of the parent."[19]

When disengaged parents or guardians come in from a long day at work their first response is to kick the proverbial dog out of frus-tration. When they do they're kicking much more than the dog (as if kicking a dog isn't sad enough). They're kicking their children's hope and optimism about their own future. Children take cues from what they see. They watch closely and listen intently. If their parents or guardians feel trapped, enslaved, or angry about their jobs, then they figure, *What hope do I have for my own future?*

Their undeveloped minds struggle to understand the logic of staying in school only to eventually enter a job they're going to hate. Perhaps this is why over eight thousand US high school students drop out *every day.*[20] They rationalize, *Why exert the energy if frustration is all I have to look forward to?*

The disengaged and actively disengaged, all 70 percent of them, cope by compartmentalizing their pain. They convince themselves they can be engaged in their "personal lives" even though they're disengaged in their "professional lives." Unfortunately, this strategy doesn't work. Who we are is who we are, *wherever* we go. If you're imprisoned at work you're not free at home. Your mind doesn't simply stay at work. It travels with you.

4. People's Lives Will Change

There's much more at stake than simply you. It's a deal that even eclipses your loved ones. Staying disengaged in your day job is quite possibly the most selfish action available. Because when you delay your dream job, you also delay life change in other people.

Sound crazy?

That thought certainly didn't cross my mind when I sat crying in my director's office back in 2010. All I could think about was my family and their needs. My mind fixated on everything I was about to give up. As much as I'd like to pretend otherwise, my thoughts weren't focused on the future readers of my books or the future members of my online programs.

Since then I've matured.

I realized that my journey is much bigger than me. I discovered that by pursuing my dream job, I injected more believability, authenticity, and credibility into myself and my message.

I didn't come to this conclusion on my own. People like Austin Miller helped me realize this. He sent me an email two days ago that made my day job to dream job switch worth it. I share this as an encouragement. Your future tribe is waiting on you. They need the transformation you'll stir within them. But they need you to embrace your dream job first.

Here's Austin's email:

> Hope you're having a great week! I wanted to say thank you again for following what God put on your heart. Because of your obedience my life has been impacted and forever changed. I appreciate your wisdom and I've loved the Thursday night **Deeper Path Coaching Cohort**. I'm glad I took the step of faith a few months ago, when I was unemployed, knowing God would provide clarity for the future steps of my life. I'm loving my new job and I'm now a soul on fire.—Austin

Reading his words humbled and encouraged me. I had no idea that by pursuing my dream job other people would also find the courage and confidence to pursue theirs. Before my day job switch I was too immature and inexperienced to see it.

If this hasn't already happened to you, it will. DJs receive unexpected affirmations from their tribe. Mike Myers is one such DJ. He and his wife saw a former client out in public the other day. The student ran up to both of them, dragging his parents with him.

"Mom! Dad! It's *him*! It's Mr. Myers . . . my tutor, the one who helped me learn how to read!"

Based on his enthusiasm, it appeared that this student had just bumped into his favorite rock star. Equally surprising were the parents' responses. Thrusting out his hand and offering a firm handshake, the father said, "Mr. Myers, you've helped our son so much. He's like a different child . . . and his confidence is unbelievable." The mother completed the circle by adding her own heartfelt compliments.

Who would have thought switching from painter to tutor would have elicited so much appreciation? Mike had no idea that pursing his dream job would change a child's future. Now, with a few years as a tutor, he's seen dozens of futures changed forever.

You can't discount your dream job. DJs never do. Check out four truths they never ignore.

Four Truths DJs Don't Ignore

1. World changers don't let themselves get in the way of changing the world.

2. Your message is even bigger than your self-limiting beliefs.
3. *Selfishness* says, "If I pursue my dream job, what will I lose?"
4. *Selflessness* says, "If I pursue my dream job, what will others gain?"

You forget these truths when you get lost in your own story. But you take your responsibility a little more seriously when you realize other people bind their dreams to your action—and your inaction.

If your message is stuck, then chances are so is your tribe. It's difficult to change someone's life if they haven't experienced your product or service.

For most people this seems like an encouraging but unbelievable thought. *Dreamers like Steve Jobs and Thomas Edison changed the world, but little old me? How could my dream job change someone else's life?*

Don't buy into the false humility act! It doesn't serve you or your tribe.

We need to hear your voice.

We need to see your passion.

We need to discover your idea.

My life changed because certain people pursued their dream job. People like my mentor, Dave Plaster, whom I met in college. He taught me how to believe. People like my high school teacher Mr. Moore. He taught me how to think. People like my wife, Kelly, a licensed counselor. She taught me how to feel.

All these people, and many more, said *yes* to their dream jobs. Will you?

5. You Will Live Longer

Although the first four reasons for starting your dream job are important, the final one could be a life-or-death issue, literally. Perhaps it all sounds a bit melodramatic, until you look at the startling data. In his breakthrough book, *48 Days to the Work You Love*, author Dan Miller reveals the brutal truth:

70 percent of American workers experience stress-related illnesses.

34 percent think they will burn out on the job in the next two years.

The *Los Angeles Times* reports that there is a 33 percent increase in heart attacks on Monday mornings.

According to the National Centers for Disease Control and Prevention, more people die at nine o'clock Monday morning than at any other time of day or any other day of the week.

Entrepreneur magazine adds that there is a 25 percent increase in work-related injuries on Mondays.

Male suicides are highest on Sunday nights, with men realizing that their careers—and possibly their finances as well—are not where they want them.[21]

Staying in your day jobs may be hazardous to your health. Maybe your *why* for leaving just got bigger—Way bigger.

5. More Instruction ("The How")

If you read this book, you can plan and implement your escape.

Harriet Tubman, escaped slave and famous conductor on the Underground Railroad, knew a powerful truth. Although incredibly successful, she commented, "I freed thousands of slaves and could have freed thousands more, if only they had known they were slaves."[22]

Regrettably, Tubman couldn't convince certain people they were slaves. Therefore she couldn't convince them of their need for escape.

It's no different today. Because of this human tendency, I've spent the first section of the book proving that day jobs hold you prisoner. If I'd started by revealing the plan for escape, you would have felt unserved.

Truth is, most people refuse to believe they're imprisoned. Sadly, they'll sit in their cells (aka cubicles) and remain prisoners for the rest of their lives.

I believe you're different.

I believe you're still with me.

I believe you're willing to explore The Dream Jobber Plan and eventually implement your own escape.

The Shawshank Inside Us All

Speaking of prison escapes, when stuck back in my day job I often thought about a particular movie—*The Shawshank Redemption*. Remember it?

Most people do . . . at least now. It's the prison movie with Tim Robbins and Morgan Freeman. Funny thing is, on some levels it's not about a prison at all. It took a little time, but the public eventually came to realize this too. And when they did its popularity soared.

Despite being nominated for seven Academy Awards when it released in 1994, the movie won none. Although reception for *The Shawshank Redemption* seemed dismal at first, barely even making budget, it eventually picked up momentum through cable television and home rental. Twenty years later, the results speak for themselves. *The Shawshank Redemption*:

Became the top rental of 1995.

Reached the rank of the highest grossing rentals of all time.[23]

Was listed in the AFI's top 100 years . . . 100 movies.[24]

Was heralded as the *It's a Wonderful Life* of its day.[25]

Secured the top movie spot of all time (as voted by the public).[26]

Why does some movie about a guy stuck in a prison garner a cultlike following even today? As pointed out by Roger Ebert in his critical review, "Mostly the film is an allegory about holding onto a sense of personal worth, despite everything."[27]

When making the switch from our day jobs to our dream jobs, you'll see amazing parallels with *Shawshank*. If you've already seen the movie, you'll benefit from a quick recap. If you haven't, understanding the plot will help you see your current situation more clearly.

The movie, which takes place in 1947, begins with banker Andy Dufresne (played by Tim Robbins) receiving two consecutive life sentences at Shawshank State Penitentiary. Convicted of murdering his wife and her lover, based on circumstantial evidence, Andy finds himself rather quickly in a brand-new world with brand-new rules.

Unfortunately, this particular world, run by a coldhearted warden, snuffs out any wisp of hope. The warden embodies a strange blend of religious hypocrisy and institutional reformation. He enjoys crushing hope out of everyone who steps out of sync with his intentionally designed culture of cruelty. The new prisoners, affectionately called "new fish," experienced this cruelty the moment they stepped in Shawshank.

Except for Andy. He seemed immune.

Despite his false imprisonment, he maintained an incredibly optimistic outlook. Choosing to rise above his circumstances, Andy had every opportunity to give up and give in. The victim of rape, abuse, and deception, Andy didn't allow circumstances to destroy him or his hope. He continued to survive and thrive mainly due to a little secret only he knew.

Andy quickly befriended a fellow inmate nicknamed "Red" (played by Morgan Freeman). This contraband smuggler and "citizen of Shawshank" knew the rules of the game. Despite serving his own life sentence, Red periodically found himself up for potential early release. Unfortunately, each time he faced the review board, they answered his attempt to define rehabilitation with the response—*rejected*.

Serving as the narrator throughout the movie, Red helps the viewer understand more about life in Shawshank and Andy's demeanor that seemed to rise above the stone-cold walls:

> He had a quiet way about him, a walk and a talk that just wasn't normal around here. He strolled. Like a man in a park without a care or worry. Like he had on an invisible coat that would shield him from this place.[28]

Andy's fellow prisoners lacked these "invisible coats," even when released. After serving fifty years in Shawshank, one convict named Brooks reentered society, quite unsuccessfully. Although free on the outside, he still suffered from a mental prison on the inside.

Unable to perform the simplest jobs like bagging groceries at a local supermarket, Brooks tells himself it's easier to end his life than try to create a new one. Red shared his perspective about Brooks's mental condition:

This place is all he knows. In here, he's an important man, an educated
man. A librarian. Out there, he's nothing but a used-up old con with
arthritis in both hands. . . . These walls are funny. First you hate 'em,
then you get used to 'em. After long enough, you get so you depend
on 'em. That's "institutionalized." . . . They send you here for life, and
that's just what they take. Part that counts, anyway.[29]

Sounds mighty similar to the bulk of Day Jobbers I've met. Even
after retirement, many still feel imprisoned by their jobs. They can't
rest, relax, or enjoy life. Although they're free on the outside, they
still suffer from a prison on the inside.

Maybe this is why Andy spread hope and humanity in an incredibly
hopeless and inhumane place. Shortly after Brooks's suicide, Andy
broke the rules. Locking himself in the same office as the public address system, Andy broadcasted a piece of music by Mozart across
the entire prison for everybody to hear—guard and prisoner alike.

Obviously impacted by Andy's rebellion, Red revealed his thoughts.
"It was like some beautiful bird flapped into our drab little cage and
made these walls dissolve away . . . and for the briefest of moments—
every last man at Shawshank felt free."[30]

Andy achieved his mission. But he also paid a horrible price—two
weeks in solitary confinement. His fellow inmates greeted him at lunch
upon his release. They imagined he would have carried a broken spirit
with his tray of food that day. To their surprise, he appeared more
impassioned and only carrying more courage.

Obviously confused, they let him know it. Andy told them it was
the easiest time he ever did because Mr. Mozart accompanied him.
Now even more confused, they thought he brought a record player
with him.

Andy: "The music was here . . . and here [tapping his head and
his heart]. That's the one thing they can't confiscate, not
ever. That's the beauty of it. Haven't you ever felt that way
about music, Red?"

Red: "Played a mean harmonica as a younger man. Lost my
taste for it. Didn't make much sense on the inside."

Andy: "Here's where it makes most sense. We need it so we don't forget."

Red: "Forget?"

Andy: "That there are things in this world not carved out of gray stone. That there's a small place inside of us they can never lock away, and that place is called hope."

Red: "Hope is a dangerous thing. Drive a man insane. It's got no use on the inside. Better get used to the idea."

Andy: "Like Brooks did?"[31]

Andy didn't back down from Red's rationale. He knew something the other prisoners didn't—*hope*. For them it was a word. For Andy it was an escape. And that's just what Andy did. He converted his attitude into action and devised a strategic escape plan.

That's what made him different. That's why he walked with a stroll. While the rest of the prisoners suffered from an internal prison, Andy knew freedom even before he tasted it. Although imprisoned on the outside, Andy was already free on the inside.

Similarly, I want to help you create an escape plan. Before I do, you'll have to admit that you're a prisoner. If you're still in denial, then I can't help. But if you want to escape your day job and enter your dream job, then I'd be honored to help you imagine and implement your own escape plan.

The Dream Jobber Plan

If you want to jailbreak your job, you need a plan. In part 2 we'll customize The Dream Jobber Plan for you and your situation. We'll explore these nine steps one at a time in detail, but for now here's a quick peek:

Step One: DESIGN Your Story
Your GPS dictates your destination.

Step Two: DESIGN Your Space
Our experience reflects your values.

Step Three: DESIGN Your Service
Choose your solution, then your service style.

Step Four: CREATE Your Platform
If you want to be heard, you must be seen.

Step Five: CREATE Your Product
Products increase influence, impact, and income.

Step Six: CREATE Your Promotion
Market before you manufacture.

Step Seven: MAINTAIN Your Community
Every dream needs a team.

Step Eight: MAINTAIN Your Clarity
Complexity kills clarity.

Step Nine: MAINTAIN Your Credibility
Success is found in singularity.

Sitting in Shawshank

I'm sitting in Shawshank prison right now, writing this book.

I made the trip to Mansfield, Ohio, to the Ohio State Reformatory—the prison used to film *The Shawshank Redemption*—with one single purpose in mind. I wanted to start off this first chapter literally inside the prison cell. I wanted the door slammed shut behind me and with it any chance of hope for escaping. I wanted to remind myself how I used to feel, completely separated from any chance at freedom.

I'm in the exact cell where Andy served solitary confinement as punishment for playing his famous anthem of freedom. Although it's June, this cramped room feels strangely cool. The lady who let me in tried to convince me that this entire prison is haunted. As if the ghost tour signs don't give me enough warning.

I'm not going to lie. It feels a little spooky. Unlike a mainstream museum, overpopulated with people, this one feels quite lonely. Come to think of it, I'm the only person in this entire block of cells. (OK, now I'm starting to scare myself.)

Trust me. These cells haven't been cleaned for decades. All the proof you need is the old, stained mattress in the cell next to mine.

It all feels so odd because the last two years I've been free. Although I'm living my dream job today, it's easy to forget how many years I spent stuck in my day job. I've vowed never to lose perspective and empathy for those still stuck.

That's why I came back.

For you.

I've seen too many causalities to stay silent. A former citizen of Shawshank, like Andy, I've since found my own Zihuatanejo.

Don't worry. Before we're done that will all make sense—including Zihuatanejo. But in the simplicity of this moment, in the words of Andy, you only have one of two choices—get busy living or get busy dying.

I hope you choose to get busy living. And if that's your choice, then keep reading—so we can get busy planning.

Key Points

(If you RT, use #DJtoDJ to join the conversation with other DJs)

1. Dream Jobbers experience freedom (go as you please), finances (earn as you wish), and fulfillment (live as you like).

2. DJs reclaim the rights over their lives by changing the rules of the game.

3. Day Jobbers work to maintain a lifestyle they can't enjoy because they're trapped in their work.

4. DJs know how to increase two things—their value in the marketplace and their passive income.

5. Raising your rates requires slaying some fairly big mental giants.

6. Your pricing says way more about your self-image than your personal value.

7. Create a business that's both passive income *and* passive impact.

8. Fear isn't the enemy. Inaction is!

9. Margins create space for life to catch up with you.

10. Our chances for success are far greater today than at any other time in human history.

11. If you know the right rules and abide by them, no one is beyond your reach.

12. If you know where to go, the world is at your fingertips, literally.

13. If you can get online, you can run your business.

14. If you don't have to stay in your day job, why would you?

15. If you read this book, you can plan and implement your escape.

PART 2

THE PLAN

Step One: DESIGN Your Story

Your GPS Dictates Your Destination

Sometimes stories cry out to be told in such loud voices that you write them just to shut them up.

Stephen King

You think in stories, and so do I.

From the earliest of times, we've retold our history through the spoken word, not the written one. Born into a story, you're naturally an expert storyteller whether you recognize it or not.

Your storytelling began with your first breath and won't stop until your heart does. As a child you told yourself stories when you heard a noise at night. *I see glowing eyes in my closet. Something is under my bed. A monster wants to eat me.*

Your parent or guardian responded with *other stories* to help calm you down. *There are no such things as monsters. It was just the wind. I will protect you.*

Your knack for storytelling sticks with you well into adulthood. Consciously and subconsciously, you tell yourself thousands of *mini narratives* every day.

You tell stories about:

Why they didn't have it in stock.

Why the waitress seemed rude.

Why the client came early.

Why the mail came late.

On topic with our conversation, you tell yourself stories about:

Why you continue to stay in your day job.

Why you fail to start your dream job.

Why the obsession with stories?

Stories wield tremendous power, helping you understand yourself and your context better. They provide three benefits.

Stories Provide

1. **Perspective**—They give you vision.
2. **Permission**—They give you consent.
3. **Promotion**—They give you visibility.

Let's unpack these one at a time.

1. Perspective—Stories Give You Vision

Without vision you can't see yourself or your world clearly. You have no framework or vantage point. But unfortunately vision isn't neutral. It comes in two versions: *incorrect vision* and *correct vision*.

Incorrect Vision

You see what can't be. You see yourself negatively with endless self-limiting beliefs. You take inventory of all the possible obstacles, challenges, and limitations.

Devil's advocates always have *incorrect vision*, and they love telling everyone else what they see. As you might expect, they're not the only ones who suffer from *incorrect vision*. You do too.

It's easy to identify. Whenever self-limiting beliefs show up, then *incorrect vision* is at work. These types of beliefs manifest themselves in thousands of *mini narratives* that sabotage your success. Yet, after working with hundreds of people, I've discovered all self-limiting beliefs center on two core lies:

I am not enough (lack of worth).

I don't have enough (lack of resources).

Obviously, operating with this story set on repeat inside your headspace produces a negative result. Check out the seven most common manifestations:

I Am Not Enough . . . (Worth)	I Don't Have Enough . . . (Resources)	Result
1. Physically	Beauty	I hide in fear.
2. Mentally	Education	I hide in fear.
3. Spiritually	Discipline	I hide in fear.
4. Emotionally	Experience	I hide in fear.
5. Financially	Money	I hide in fear.
6. Intellectually	Brains	I hide in fear.
7. Relationally	Friends	I hide in fear.

Both lies (I am not enough/I don't have enough) center on *lack*. Rather than reflecting abundance, they reflect scarcity. You might wonder, where did this scarcity mindset originate? Like all beliefs, it stems from stories too. Let's revisit just one. Maybe you've heard this particular scarcity story as a child:

The early bird gets the worm.

Usually, a well-meaning adult relayed this story to you to motivate you to action. Innocent? Seemingly.

Until you unpack the proposition. Let's focus on the two main characters in this ultrashort yet influential story: the worm and the bird. First the worm.

Notice, *the* worm?

As if there's only *one* worm in the entire world? Last time I checked, billions of worms populated the earth. Grab a shovel and start digging anywhere and you'll find more worms than you ever wanted. A quick search on Google reveals thousands of videos and websites devoted to starting your own worm farming business.[1]

The worm?

Try more than 4,400 species of worms already discovered, classified, and named by scientists![2]

Now, notice the *early* bird.

In our short story, why must birds compete against each another? Can't they form teams or families? Last time I checked, birds live in community and work toward a common goal. Besides, *early* signifies a race. What about the punctual bird who showed up on time? Is it disqualified?

Fast-forward twenty years and examine those children who believed the *early bird gets the worm* scarcity story. What do you observe in people who retell that story a thousand times over?

You end up with adults who believe:

They must compete with everyone else for limited resources.

Fear must drive their attitudes and actions.

Other people need to lose just so they can win.

How many people in your world suffer from *incorrect vision?* How many see what *can't be?* How many see themselves negatively with endless self-limiting beliefs? How many fail to take inventory of all the possible obstacles, challenges, and limitations?

Easier question: How many *don't?*

Only those with *correct vision.*

Correct Vision

You see what could be. You see yourself positively with nearly unlimited potential. You take inventory of all the possible opportunities, advantages, and incentives.

Seeing correctly yields tremendous benefits for yourself and those around you. Although shifting from *incorrect* to *correct* might seem difficult, it's definitely possible.

Consider Dr. Howard Hendricks, a former professor at Dallas

Theological Seminary. He began with *incorrect vision*, but all that changed through a conversation with an elementary school teacher:

> "I was born into a broken home," the 78-year-old man says. "My parents separated when I came along. I split the family."
>
> Reared by his father's mother, Dr. Hendricks says that in elementary school he was a troublemaker, a hell raiser. Probably just acting out a lot of insecurities, he says looking back on his Philadelphia childhood. His fifth-grade teacher had predicted that five boys in class would end up in prison. He was supposed to be one of them. The teacher was right about three of them, Dr. Hendricks says. That teacher, Miss Simon, once tied him to his seat with a rope and taped his mouth shut.
>
> When he introduced himself to his sixth-grade teacher, Miss Noe, she told him something that would change his life forever.
>
> "She said, 'I've heard a lot about you, but I don't believe a word of it,'" he recalls.
>
> She made him realize for the first time in his life that someone cared, he says. "People are always looking for someone to say, 'Hey, I believe in you.'"
>
> In his 52 years as a professor at Dallas Seminary, that's what he has sought to do—believe in his students and help develop them.[3]

Dr. Hendricks shifted from negative, self-limiting beliefs to positive, unlimited potential. Rather than joining three fellow classmates in a life of crime, he created a new life instead.

Miss Noe helped. She told him a new story he'd never heard before. Rather than dismissing it, he let it sink in. Her story became his story, giving him a new perspective and a higher vision of what could be.

His results changed because his story changed. Dramatic events soon followed. He went from being bound to a chair so he would *shut up* to serving as department chair so he would *speak up*. By shifting to *correct vision*, Dr. Hendricks trained some of the best and brightest professionals in his field for more than half a century. His students went on to lead some of the largest and most influential churches in the world.

Shift Your Results with the Story Shift

In Dr. Hendrick's example, we see a powerful principle. I call this the Story Shift. It happens when you change your results by changing your story. Here's another way of picturing it:

Stories > Beliefs > Thoughts > Feelings > Actions > Results

Let's explore this phenomenon with a common example—a salesperson producing poor results.

Imagine this salesperson, named Wendy, isn't selling enough widgets. She'll be fired if she can't make a quick turnaround. If Wendy wants different **results** she needs to change her **actions.**

With a little digging we find out she loves doing product demos, but she hates calling companies to set them up. For the sake of simplicity, let's imagine calling companies is the only way to set up the demos. Clearly, she needs to overcome her fears to change her undesirable results.

We know she **feels** fear when making calls, but why?

Turns out Wendy **thinks** companies won't want to talk to her. She **believes** they already have their act together and don't need her help. As a result, she's told herself a powerful but untrue **story.** She's convinced herself she's *that* girl. *That* clueless girl who's a pest. *That* girl they hang up on and gossip about at water coolers.

In summary, every time Wendy attempts to call a company she tells herself a debilitating story about being *that* girl. Her story creates a belief that she's annoying and inconveniencing the company. She thinks they'll hang up on her. Her feelings of fear prevent her from taking action and making the call. But without the call, she never gets the opportunity to prove herself at the demo. The result is a disaster—no sales!

Let's compare the results when Wendy applies the Story Shift:

Imagine Wendy changes her **story.** Instead of telling herself she's *that* girl, she now tells herself she's the answer to their prayers. She **believes** the company she's about to call is in a desperate situation. They've reached a wall and their staff is at a crossroads. People are ready to walk because of the crisis at hand.

Wendy focuses her **thinking** on their need for her product rather than her own self-limiting beliefs. She **feels** emboldened and empowered to serve them with all the expertise she possesses.

With newfound passion she takes action and dials the phone. Wendy embodies an incredibly unique blend of presence and enthusiasm. Impressed with her confidence and competence, the company immediately schedules a demo. After nine more phone calls she schedules five additional demos. The final **results**? Later that week, she closes five of her six demos. Quite easily, she outperforms her fellow salespeople who previously held the record with a 50 percent close rate.

By changing her story, Wendy changed her results. She applied the Story Shift and became a superstar salesperson in the process. Her new story gave her *correct vision* and she quickly saw the unlimited potential of what could be.

Wendy took inventory of all the possible opportunities, advantages, and incentives around her. Surprisingly they always existed. She just needed a new story to give her a new perspective.

2. Permission—Stories Give Us Consent

Without consent you don't take action. You play safe and play small because your default is to avoid risk. At least *intentional* risk.

As a toddler you risked your life for a cookie. Standing on a counter four feet off the ground and leaning precariously to reach the jar seemed brilliant at the time. But chalk up that action as blind ignorance. Once you fail a time or two, you quickly learn how falling on your backside truly feels. Settling for inaction seems better for your backside and your ego.

Regardless, stories *can* change all this. A quick look at history helps you see how stories gave people permission to take action.

Queen Esther issued a story with a proclamation that inspired a three-day fast in hopes of saving her entire nation.

JFK told a story about landing a man on the moon that escalated the Space Race.

Martin Luther King Jr. shared a story with his "I Have a Dream" speech that fueled the civil rights movement.

Al Gore presented a story through a documentary that increased global awareness about climate change.

Before hearing their respective stories, the Jews, Americans, activists, and environmentalists already knew their cause. But their stories gave them consent. They inspired them because they gave them permission to take even more action.

Your story contains the same potential. Shifting from your day job to your dream job is just as dramatic and just as epic. Doubting this truth only fuels inaction.

When you discount your dream, you merely announce your own ignorance. As we examined in the previous chapter, if you don't permit your dream job to advance, many lives will remain unchanged.

Your Story—Your Responsibility

Investing time with hundreds of Day Jobbers and Dream Jobbers alike, I've observed three main responses regarding our stories.

Response	Posture	Action	Tribe
Defer Your Story	Put Off	No Action	Day Jobber
Destroy Your Story	Put Down	Negative Action	Day Jobber
Design Your Story	Put Forth	Positive Action	Dream Jobber

DEFER YOUR STORY

The majority of people postpone their stories for another day. Their motive? They believe indecision has its advantages because choosing a side requires work and risk.

Reminds me of a scene from *The Matrix*. Neo visits a woman named the Oracle to find out if he's "the One." If she identifies him as such then he is accountable for saving the world. If she tells him he's not "the One," then he's off the hook.

Oracle: "Do you think you are the One?"

Neo: "Honestly, I don't know."

Neo refuses to take a position or exert any *action*. He feels comfortable *deferring* and making others do the tough work for him. However, the Oracle refused to play his game. She makes him pick a side.

Oracle: "OK, now I'm supposed to say, 'Hmm, that's interesting, but . . .' then you say . . ."

Neo: ". . . but what?"

Oracle: "But . . . you already know what I'm going to tell you."

Neo: "I'm not the One."

Oracle: "Sorry, kid. You got the gift, but it looks like you're waiting for something."

Neo: "What?"

Oracle: "Your next life, maybe. Who knows? That's the way these things go."[4]

The Oracle simply acted as a mirror, reflecting Neo's unbelief right back at him. She never said he wasn't "the One," but she let him know he was waiting for something. She made it clear he was *putting off* his story.

Day Jobbers defer their stories because it seems easier. Maya Angelou observed, "*There is no greater agony than bearing an untold story inside you.*"[5] Putting off your story doesn't solve your problem; it only prolongs your pain.

DESTROY YOUR STORY

Live long enough and you realize it's simpler to break something than to build it—including yourself. Tragically, many people *destroy* their own stories intentionally. Take your pick: sports, entertainment, or music—every week somebody else puts down their own story through negative action. We saw this destruction in sports with Brett Favre, entertainment with Lindsay Lohan, and music with Kurt Cobain.[6]

For those unfamiliar with Kurt Cobain, he functioned as the lead singer, guitarist, and primary songwriter of the grunge band Nirvana. *Rolling Stone* magazine identified Nirvana as "the flagship band" of Generation X and Cobain was hailed as "the spokesman of a generation."[7] They sold over fifty million albums; few other bands have ever reached such a high level of popularity and success. But instead of enjoying his story, Cobain destroyed it.

On April 8, 1994, at age twenty-seven, Cobain was found dead at his home in Seattle. His death was officially ruled a suicide, resulting from a self-inflicted shotgun wound to the head. His suicide letter invites you into his story.

> *I haven't felt the excitement of listening to as well as creating music along with reading and writing for too many years now. I feel guilty beyond words about these things. For example when we're backstage and the lights go out and the manic roar of the crowd begins, it doesn't affect me the way in which it did for Freddie Mercury, who seemed to love, relish in the love and adoration from the crowd, which is something I totally admire and envy.*
>
> *The fact is, I can't fool you, any one of you. It simply isn't fair to you or me. The worst crime I can think of would be to rip people off by faking it and pretending as if I'm having 100% fun. Sometimes I feel as if I should have a punch-in time clock before I walk out on stage. I've tried everything within my power to appreciate it.*
>
> *. . . I appreciate the fact that I and we have affected and entertained a lot of people. I need to be slightly numb in order to regain the enthusiasm I once had as a child . . . I can't stand the thought of Frances (daughter) becoming the miserable, self-destructive, death rocker that I've become. I have it good, very good, and I'm grateful.*
>
> *. . . I don't have the passion anymore, and so remember, it's better to burn out than to fade away.*
>
> *Peace, love, empathy,*
> *Kurt Cobain*

Frances and Courtney (wife), I'll be at your altar.
Please keep going Courtney, for Frances.
For her life, which will be so much happier without me.[8]

Just a troubled soul? Maybe. But more than other Day Jobbers? Notice the key phrases:

"I haven't felt the excitement."

"The crowd . . . doesn't affect me."

"Faking . . . and pretending as if I'm having 100 percent fun."

"Sometimes I feel as if I should have a punch-in time clock."

"I've tried everything within my power to appreciate it."

"I need to be slightly numb in order to regain the enthusiasm I once had."

"I don't have the passion anymore."

"It's better to burn out than to fade away."

Day Jobbers utter those exact words. Maybe not out loud, but certainly in their heads.

Maybe Cobain isn't much different from you. He may have literally pulled the trigger, but how many Day Jobbers are already dead?

What's better? To die instantly? Or to die slowly throughout your career?

To lose your life with one action? Or to lose your heart with a thousand tiny compromises?

Day Jobbers destroy their stories because it seems easier. Ivan Klíma observed, "To destroy is easier than to create . . . but what would they say if one asked them what they wanted instead?"[9] Putting down your story doesn't help your cause; it only hurts your legacy.

Design Your Story

To join the DJs you must *design your story.* Forget deferring or destroying—that's for Day Jobbers. DJs *put forth* their stories with clarity and confidence by taking *positive action.*

Here's a quick refresher.

To escape your day job *prison* you need a dream job *plan*. And your particular plan includes nine critical steps. The first step in The Dream Jobber Plan is to *design your story*. The other eight steps depend on the quality of this first one.

Here's why—*your story dictates your destination*.

Hang with me thirty more seconds and I'll reframe the way you see your story and maybe even the way you see yourself.

Meet the Five Types of Gurus

You might not see yourself as a guru (and that's part of the problem). But after reading the definition, you no longer have a choice. Time to accept the truth—you're a guru. A guru is:

> A *teacher and especially intellectual guide in matters of fundamental concern.*
>
> *One who is an acknowledged leader or chief proponent.*
>
> A *person with knowledge or expertise.*[10]

Like most humans on the big blue rock, you probably doubt your guru status. Not many people wear robes and conduct eloquent pontifications in their spare time—but gurus look quite different these days. Here's the five different guru clans:

Clans	Deliverable	Probability
Practicals	Personal Results	100%
Synthesizers	Relevant Themes	75%
Nonconformists	Uncommon Perspectives	50%
Academics	Research/Data	25%
Celebrities	Familiar Endorsements	less than 1%

Let's examine the unique characteristics of each.

THE PRACTICALS

These gurus deliver personal results. They've climbed the mountain, built the business, cracked the code. Rather than sharing theory, these gurus share from their own experience. Their content feels authentic, chock-full of struggle and victory. Think: hero's journey retold.

Example of a Practical:

Arthur Boorman is a former military paratrooper with over two hundred jumps to his credit. When he returned home from the Gulf War, military doctors told Arthur what his body was already telling him—his assortment of injuries that had ravaged his legs, back, jaw, and wrist had resulted in the end of his military career. He would never walk unassisted, without a cane or walker, again.

As a special education teacher working seventy to eighty hours a week, he found that his transition into civilian life coupled with his constant pain resulted in putting on well over forty pounds his first year out of the service. His weight had ballooned to 340 pounds by a few years later.

At age forty-seven, Arthur was headed to an early grave. With the thought of not being around for his wife of almost thirty years and their three sons, he made the decision to take control of his life. After two yoga studios turned him away, he discovered DDP yoga, invented by professional wrestling heavyweight champion "Diamond" Dallas Page. The zero-impact, high-energy, fat-burning workout helped Arthur shed 140 pounds in ten months.

Arthur's YouTube video featuring his transformation went viral (over ten million hits and counting). His testimony inspires and motivates others to own their lives, take control, never give up—and get healthy.[11]

Iowa City Yoga Festival listed him as one of their keynote speakers. Doubters take note: Boorman has "stretched his way" to guru status.

The Synthesizers

These gurus deliver relevant themes. They've booked the interviews, explored the best practices, and synthesized the results. Rather than regurgitating traditional dogma, these gurus serve up fresh perspectives based on emerging trends. Their content feels innovative, robust, and original. Think: obvious epiphany.

Example of a Synthesizer:

Malcolm Gladwell has been a staff writer with the *New Yorker* magazine since 1996. He wrote *The Tipping Point*, *Blink*, and *Outliers*—all of which were number one *New York Times* bestsellers.

From 1987 to 1996, he was a reporter with the *Washington Post*, where he covered business and science, and then served as the newspaper's New York City bureau chief. He graduated from the University of Toronto, Trinity College, with a degree in history. He was born in England, grew up in rural Ontario, and now lives in New York City.

In his first book, *The Tipping Point*, Gladwell suggests that word of mouth phenomena shares similar characteristics with epidemics. Ideas, products, messages, and behaviors spread just like viruses do. He proves his proposition with examples from various sectors of society such as history (Paul Revere), entertainment (*Sesame Street* and *Blue's Clues*), and commerce (Hush Puppies Shoes).[12]

In 2005 *Time* magazine named him one of the "100 Most Influential People." Clearly, Gladwell "wrote the book" on guru status.

THE NONCONFORMISTS

These gurus deliver uncommon perspectives. They've examined opinion, etiquette, and outlook and dared to stand in defiance. Rather than marching in line, these gurus chart their own course. Their content feels unconventional, raw, and passionate. Think: brace yourself, hear it comes.

Example of a Nonconformist:
In his own words, Dave Ramsey has an unusual way of looking at the world.

My wife, Sharon, says I'm weird and truthfully—I am weird. But there's a reason. Starting from nothing, by the time I was 26 I had a net worth of a little over a million dollars. I was making $250,000 a year—that's more than $20,000 a month net taxable income. I was really having fun. But 98% truth is a lie, and that 2% can cause big problems, especially with $4 million in real estate. I had a lot of debt—a lot of short-term debt—and I'm the idiot who signed up for the trip.

After losing everything, I went on a quest to find out how money really works, how I could get control of it and how I could have confidence in handling it. I read everything I could get my hands on. I interviewed older rich people, people who made money and kept it. That quest led me to a really, really uncomfortable place: my mirror. I came to realize that my money problems, worries and shortages largely began and ended with the person in my mirror. I also realized that if

I could learn to manage the character I shaved with every morning, I would win with money.

I formed The Lampo Group in 1992 to counsel folks hurting from the results of financial stress. I've paid the "stupid tax" (mistakes with dollar signs on the end) so hopefully some of you won't have to. I wrote the book, *Financial Peace*, based on all that Sharon and I had learned, and I began selling it out of my car. With a friend of mine, I started a local radio call-in show called *The Money Game*, now nationally syndicated as *The Dave Ramsey Show*.

Many companies define success based on the dollars coming in, but at The Lampo Group, we define our success by the number of lives changed: listeners getting out of debt, readers taking their first Baby Step and saving $1,000, FPU graduates investing for their future. We learned early on that if we help enough people, the money will come. Our mission statement isn't just lip service—it's our mantra.

The Lampo Group, Inc. is providing biblically based, common-sense education and empowerment which gives HOPE to everyone from the financially secure to the financially distressed.[13]

Ramsey has been featured on many media outlets including *The Oprah Winfrey Show*, *60 Minutes*, *The Early Show on CBS*, *Fox Business Network*, *Dr. Phil*, and many more.[14] Ramsey has undoubtedly "banked" guru status.

The Academics

These gurus deliver data. They've earned the degrees, written the papers, and conducted the experiments. Rather than personal opinion, these gurus share from a deep reservoir of science and research. Their content feels proven, credible, and plausible. Think: graduate class.

Example of an Academic:

Oliver Sacks, MD, is a physician, a bestselling author, and a professor of neurology at the NYU School of Medicine.[15]

He is best known for his collections of neurological case histories, including *The Man Who Mistook His Wife for a Hat*, *Musicophilia: Tales of Music and the Brain*, and *The Mind's Eye*. His book *Awakenings* (1973) introduces a group of patients who had survived the great encephalitis lethargica, or "sleepy sickness," epidemic of the early twentieth century.

Maybe you skipped his book but saw the movie? Thousands did. *Awakenings* inspired the 1990 Academy Award–nominated feature film starring Robert De Niro and Robin Williams. Dr. Sacks says, "These patients 'have some words somewhere,' but must be 'tricked or seduced into discovering them.'"[16]

Dr. Sacks is a frequent contributor to the *New Yorker* and the *New York Review of Books*, and a fellow of the American Academy of Arts and Letters as well as the American Academy of Arts and Sciences. The *New York Times* has referred to him as "the poet laureate of medicine."

Translation? Dr. Sacks "aced the class" on guru status.

THE CELEBRITIES

These gurus deliver familiar endorsements. They've found their place in our conversations, status updates, and news stations. Rather than knowledge or expertise, these gurus (and their sponsors) rely on notoriety and name recognition. Their content feels reliable, trustworthy, and recognizable. Think: recommendation from a friend.

Example of a Celebrity:

Former NBA superstar Michael Jordan earned an estimated eighty million dollars in 2012 from corporate partners. According to *Forbes*, "Jordan out-earns almost every member of the world-highest paid athletes even 10 years after his last NBA game."[17]

The article continues, "The Jordan Brand is doing 'exceptionally well' says Christopher Svezia. He estimates the brand grew 25–30 percent in 2012 and now generates more than $1.75 billion globally, including apparel. The United States Jordan Brand sneaker business alone had $1.25 billion in wholesale revenue in 2012, says Matt Powell, an analyst at SportsOneSource."[18]

No one believes Michael Jordan possesses guru knowledge about all the products he endorses. How could anyone be an expert in shoes (Nike), beverages (Gatorade), underwear (Hanes), trading cards (Upper Deck), video games (2K Sports), health care (Presbyterian Healthcare), cologne (Five Star Fragrances), restaurants, and car dealerships? Clearly, these brands capitalize on Jordan's "global fame" rather than his "product intellect." Yet no one can argue with the effectiveness of his endorsements.

Forbes estimates his net worth at $650 million thanks to years of endorsement checks and $90 million in salary from the Bulls. As a celebrity, Jordan's numbers prove he "cashed in" on his guru status.

Your GPS Dictates Your Destination

I like my GPS. It helps me understand where I'm going. According to Garmin, "The Global Positioning System (GPS) is a satellite-based navigation system made up of a network of 24 satellites placed into orbit by the United States Department of Defense."[19]

Our smartphones contain GPS technology and so do our car navigation devices. Those age-old jokes about men refusing to stop and ask for directions no longer apply. With a GPS, we're without excuse if we end up lost.

DJs like their GPS too, but a different type. In our specific conversation, GPS stands for **Guru Positioning Story**.

Every DJ has one, and the best DJs position theirs well for maximum effectiveness. This unique story serves as the key factor in dictating their final destination. They integrate their GPS into everything they do, including the clan they join.

Choose Your Guru Clan

For now, simply choose which guru clan you identify with the most. Keep in mind, out of the five clans, *practicals* are the easiest to join, followed by *synthesizers*, *nonconformists*, *academics*, and then *celebrities*.

In honor of your time, I'll devote the most space explaining how to join the practical and synthesizer guru clans. (Why invest time talking about celebrities when less than 1 percent of us join them?)

PRACTICALS

Most people underestimate their own expertise. You undervalue yourself because you know of someone who knows more than you do.

Think of your hobby for a moment. Chances are you're aware of someone in your industry who's amazing. Chances are you think that because this guru gets better results, no one will pay you.

Not true.

Tim Ferriss, author of *The 4-Hour Workweek*, says "If you aren't an expert, don't sweat it." He continues his thesis by explaining the true definition of an expert. "First, 'expert' in the context of selling product means that you know more about the product than the purchaser. No more. It is not necessary to be the best—just better than a small target number of your prospective customers."[20]

I've seen this in my own experience. I remember one weekend helping my dad create a website for his business—The New Man Project.[21] Aware that millions and millions of people knew more than me about websites, I was embarrassed by my *lack* of expertise.

Yet, after about an hour of hacking away, my dad was blown away by my knowledge of WordPress and websites. He was thrilled with his website; it achieves his goal and serves his business model.

Compared to his technological knowledge, I'm a guru.

Funny thing is the tables turned later that afternoon when it came time for us to install a new door in my house. As a former carpenter, my dad is clearly a stud (no pun intended) when it comes to home improvement.

Then there's me. Let's just say those skills skipped a generation.

After a short time, I was blown away how quickly *we* (more like *he*) installed the door. Sure, he might not be Mike Holmes from the HGTV program *Holmes on Homes*, but he's Mike Oberbrunner. Compared to my home improvement knowledge, he's a guru.

The truth is your potential client doesn't know the top guru in your industry. They know you (and remember you're a guru too). Besides, even if they knew this other guru, his or her fee is too high.

Although some top gurus create inexpensive video training, they restrict access to them personally. You can thank laws of success for this. Bestselling leadership author Andy Stanley says, "The more successful you are as a leader, the less accessible you will become."[22]

Your clear advantage over that #1 guru is your anonymity—therefore, your access.

Let me illustrate another way. The other day I went swimming with my kids at the beach. My son Keegan looked at me and said, "Dad, you have big muscles. Someday can you teach me how to work out?" I kindly thanked him for his compliment and assured him when he surpassed the age of eight we'd start our routine together.

Honestly though, a wave of shame came over me. I'll let you in on the subsequent inner dialogue that followed inside my subconscious. (Think of the Gollum scene when he talks to himself in *Lord of the Rings: The Two Towers*.)

Mean Kary—"If Keegan saw an old picture of Arnold Schwarzenegger, he'd really see some muscles. He wouldn't be impressed with me."

Nice Kary—"Yeah, but if Keegan wanted access to Arnold, he'd have to cough up a few million dollars."

Mean Kary—"Yeah, but Keegan could buy one of his old workout videos someday. Those are inexpensive and they travel easy."

Nice Kary—"Yeah, but then he wouldn't be able to receive personal attention and encouragement."

Mean Kary—"Yeah, but I am sure Arnold has better technique and could provide better results."

Nice Kary—"Yeah, but Keegan could cheat without Arnold knowing. Live training provides accountability. And Arnold doesn't even love or care for Keegan like I do."

Funny, how I had a conversation with myself about how I can outperform Arnold Schwarzenegger when it comes to caring and loving my son.

Am I crazy? (Don't answer that question.) Maybe I am.

However, did you notice all the "yeah, buts?"

Do they sound familiar?

Do you find yourself engaging in this internal dialogue too?

Do you talk yourself out of your guru status because your results don't outperform others in your industry?

Think of this in another context. If your goal is to make it down a rapids-filled river, you'll trust a guide who's done it safely a dozen times prior. The #1 world-class guide may do it faster or better, but you don't care nor could you afford him or her.

Stop denying your guru status and start embracing it. You're already part of the *practicals* guru clan. You just need to own it and position your story well.

SYNTHESIZERS

If you can read this sentence then you can join this clan. I'll show you how. Brendon Burchard provides a paradigm shifting illustration in his #1 *New York Times* bestselling book *The Millionaire Messenger*.

> If you were about to invest in real estate, would you take advice from someone who never owned a home or commercial property?
>
> Most people reply, "Absolutely not." But then I ask, "But what if that person who had never owned a property had interviewed in detail the top 20 billionaire real estate investors in the world and distilled all their lessons into a 10-step system? Would you listen then?"
>
> If someone has researched a given topic and broken it down for us, we will listen. And we will pay for their guidance.[23]

Synthesizers understand they don't need to have *been there and done that* to speak confidently on a subject. If so, then shows like *20/20, 60 Minutes, Dateline,* and *Good Morning America* wouldn't survive. What makes these programs credible is their ability to synthesize information. In a single episode, experts from various sectors weigh in with their most relevant content.

Nearly everyone can join the synthesizer clan too. Many deny my prediction by taking inventory of what they don't "have." (Isn't it interesting how we argue for that which we don't want?) We say:

"I don't have a television channel."

(You can create a YouTube account—free.)

"I don't have access to press releases."

(You can start a Twitter account—free.)

"I don't have someone to publish my content."
(You can begin a blog on WordPress—free.)

"I can't interview the top twenty experts in my industry."
(You can synthesize the best articles via the internet—free.)

These apparent obstacles are only poor excuses. Remember, you're fully resourced. You can join the synthesizers in less than thirty days. I've helped other DJs do this by using my three quick steps.

Three Steps to Join the Synthesizer Clan

1. **Choose**—Obtain the best content.
2. **Synthesize**—Combine to form new truth.
3. **Communicate**—Broadcast your message.

1. CHOOSE—*Obtain the Best Content*

Don't read everything. Your brain will blow up. Only consume the best content. According to Tim Ferriss, "If you read and understand the three top-selling books . . . you will know more about that topic than 80 percent of the readership."[24]

Not happy being in the top 20 percent?

Internet marketer Ryan Deiss tells you how to climb higher. "Buy and read at least 3 top books on your subject, and read all the blog posts for the last 60 days for the top 6 blogs in your market . . . by the time you're finished you'll be more knowledgeable than 95 percent of the people in your market . . . including most other published authors."[25]

Find the best content on your topic by visiting an online bookstore. Bestsellers are a great place to start. Check out a few reviews, click to look inside. Examine the table of contents and read an excerpt.

Next utilize a feature found on most online bookstores. They'll suggest other similar books: "If you like that book, then check out this other book." Purchase three to five of them. (I choose hard copies for a reason. But more on this in a moment.)

After placing your order, examine the top articles and blogs. Work smarter, not harder. The internet is massive, so utilize a website called Alltop. Think of Alltop as the "online magazine rack" of the web.

The purpose of Alltop is to help you answer the question, "What's happening?" in "all the topics" that interest you. We do this by collecting the headlines of the latest stories from the best sites and blogs that cover a topic. We group these collections—"aggregations"—into individual web pages. Then we display the five most recent headlines of the information sources as well as their first paragraph. Our topics run from adoption to zoology with photography, food, science, religion, celebrities, fashion, gaming, sports, politics, automobiles, Macintosh, and hundreds of other subjects along the way.

We've subscribed to thousands of sources to provide "aggregation without aggravation." To be clear, Alltop pages are starting points—they are not destinations per se. Ultimately, our goal is to enhance your online reading by displaying stories from sources that you're already visiting plus helping you discover sources that you didn't know existed.[26]

After securing the best books and the top blog posts and articles, prepare to synthesize.

2. SYNTHESIZE—*Combine to Form New Truth*

In the words of King Solomon, "There is nothing new under the sun."[27] Thousands of years later Bono sang (or stole from King Solomon), "Every poet is a thief."[28]

Bottom line? All art, discovery, and creativity must thank those who've come before. No matter how "original" your work seems, on some levels it's repackaged inspiration.

Be propelled by this, not paralyzed. You should feel liberated to create and communicate your work. But before you get started, refresh yourself with the definition of synthesis. Synthesis is:

The combining of separate elements or substances to form a coherent whole. The combination . . . whereby a new and higher level of truth is produced.[29]

Although the definition of synthesis might sound complex, the actual process is quite easy. I synthesize often. Read below to see my model or check out the free video at DayJobToDreamJob.com/resources.[30]

I call my process RSSS (Really Simple Synthesis Strategy). Here's the nine steps:

1. **Skim**—Skim the best content on your topic (top three to five books and articles/blogs).
2. **Create**—Create a brand-new "original" outline using chapter titles or steps.
3. **Write**—Write a two-sentence description for each chapter title or step.
4. **Assign**—Assign a sticky note color for each chapter title or step.
5. **Reread**—Reread the best content and place the respective color sticky note inside the book at the appropriate section that contains the relevant content.
6. **Choose**—After completing the reading, choose a mindmapping software to categorize your sticky notes. Use your chapter titles or steps as main headers. Put relevant content from your sticky notes under each header.
7. **Weave**—Write your new work! Weave in your GPS (Guru Positioning Story) and include personal illustrations.
8. **Maintain**—Maintain integrity. Don't plagiarize. If you quote, let your readers know the sources of your information.
9. **Achieve**—Achieve your goal. Deliver relevant themes. Rather than regurgitating traditional dogma, serve up fresh perspectives based on emerging trends. Your content feels innovative, robust, and original. Think of it as an obvious epiphany.

After synthesizing using the RSSS process, prepare to communicate.

3. COMMUNICATE—*Broadcast Your Message*

Choose your venue. Because you have a worldwide television channel, unlimited press releases, and a worldwide publisher, your excuses no longer hold weight. In the upcoming Dream Jobber steps, I'll explain much more about effective and efficient communication.

NONCONFORMISTS

We join the *nonconformist* clan many times by accident. If you look at the world long enough you'll probably see injustice and unbalance—most people do. But nonconformists do something more than just notice it. They speak up.

We applaud their action and congratulate their courage. While the masses sit sidelined by silence, nonconformists stand up and shout out. Throughout history, they not only cursed the darkness but also lit a candle. They not only told us what they're against but also showed us what they're for.

Sink your teeth into sixty seconds of nonconformists via the Apple "Think Different" advertising campaign. Debuting on September 28, 1997, it marked the beginning of Apple's renaissance period and was credited with setting Apple back on course. I'll warn you, though, it's convicting because it kills apathy and eliminates excuses. Although you can check out the video free online, I've included the text below:

> Here's to the crazy ones.
> The misfits.
> The rebels.
> The troublemakers.
> The round pegs in the square holes.
> The ones who see things differently.
> They're not fond of rules, and they have no respect for the status quo.
> You can quote them, disagree with them, glorify, or vilify them.
> About the only thing you can't do is ignore them.
> Because they change things.
> They push the human race forward.
> And while some may see them as the crazy ones, we see genius.
> Because the people who are crazy enough to think they can change the world
> Are the ones who DO![31]

This one-minute commercial featured black-and-white footage of seventeen iconic twentieth-century personalities. All were nonconformists. Steve Jobs, the cofounder of Apple and the narrator of this commercial, typified the nonconformist clan.

ACADEMICS

As you might expect, joining the *academic* clan requires schooling. Lots of it. As someone who earned a bachelor's degree, a master's degree, and a doctorate, I can genuinely say I respect formalized education. Many of my former professors have aided me in my journey of personal growth.

Most often, joining the academic clan requires making large investments of time and money. This clan grants credibility to the few who prove themselves over an extended time. Insiders readily acknowledge that universities operate according to bureaucracy, tenure, and "publish or perish" realities. (Blogs often don't count in this world.)

For this reason there's only a 25 percent probability of joining this clan. Keep in mind that the majority of academics don't experience large amounts of *direct* influence or *direct* income. They train a limited number of students and receive little financial compensation in return. Napoleon Hill, author of *Think and Grow Rich*, revealed this phenomenon many decades ago:

> There are two kinds of knowledge. One is general, the other is specialized. General knowledge, no matter how great in quantity or variety it may be, is of but little use in the accumulation of money. The faculties of the great universities possess, in the aggregate, practically every form of general knowledge known to civilization. *Most of the professors have but little or no money.* They specialize on *teaching* knowledge, but they do not specialize on the organization, or the *use* of knowledge.[32]

Educators are some of the best people on the planet. But remember, we're not debating that point. Within our conversation, it's important to note that the bulk of academics will never achieve guru status because their clan won't allow it. This particular clan reserves elite status for only a few.

Like all professionals, academics fit somewhere in the Influence/Income Scale. Society compensates people based on the value they provide. If your content is simply theoretical then you'll be compensated with little direct influence or income.

Comparatively, if your content is transcendent, you'll be compensated with much influence or income. Take Mother Teresa, for example. Although she received little income, her influence outpaced many renowned world leaders. Notice the scale below:

Component	Compensation	Example
Transcendent	$$$$	Spiritual Guides
Transformational	$$$	Business Coaches
Tactical	$$	Managers
Theoretical	$	Educators

CELEBRITIES

Thankfully a Google search doesn't list any schools on how to become a celebrity. (Perhaps there's an open market for this? Let's hope not.)

If you truly want to join the *celebrity* clan, then you need to do the world a favor and set yourself apart by becoming exceptional at something. (Or if you're into reality television you can become exceptional at nothing and join the clan too . . . for fifteen minutes of fame.)

Promotion Stories Give Us Visibility

Besides providing us with perspective and permission, stories also provide promotion. At least the "sticky" ones do, anyway.

According to the market research firm Yankelovich, the average city dweller sees more than five thousand ads every day. Each ad is a kind of *mini narrative* competing for your attention.

Your brain adapts by tuning out most of these stories. The only stories it allows to survive are the "sticky" ones—those that elicit one of the responses below.

Sticky Stories Cause People To

1. See themselves—They're relatable.
2. Free themselves—They're liberating.
3. Be themselves—They're authentic.
4. Pee themselves—They're memorable.

In my Dream Job Bootcamp I help my clients write their own "sticky" stories and position them successfully both in their minds and in their marketplace. For the sake of space, I'm not going to expound on these sticky stories here. However, I've provided free detailed examples of each at DayJobToDreamJob.com/resources. When you go there you'll meet a high school dropout turned entrepreneur millionaire (see yourself), a female author who overcame childhood rape (free yourself), a famous actress who battled the Imposter Syndrome (be yourself), and a shocking movie for reasons you wouldn't expect (pee yourself). It's an online experience stuffed full of education and entertainment.

Stories Need Space to Breathe

Your GPS will only thrive in an appropriate space. In the next chapter you'll meet a man named Mark who designed a space so effective that his day job couldn't help but support his transition, and for more than a year encouraged his slow departure into his dream job. Rather than arguing for him to stay, they saw the potential of his plan and answered with affirmation.

In the *Shawshank Redemption*, Andy escaped his prison by sliding through five hundred yards of sewer pipe. Mark surprisingly escaped his prison by walking out the front door.

His magic key?

He knew his story needed space to breathe. And rather than finding the correct space, he did something even better.

He designed it.

Key Points

(If you RT, use #DJtoDJ to join the conversation with other DJs)

1. Born into a story, you're naturally an expert storyteller whether you recognize it or not.

2. Stories provide perspective (vision), permission (consent), and promotion (visibility).

3. Vision comes in two versions—*incorrect vision* and *correct vision.*

4. Self-limiting beliefs center on two core lies—*I am not enough* (lack of worth) and *I don't have enough* (lack of resources).

5. By changing your story, you can change your results.

6. The Story Shift = Stories > Beliefs > Thoughts > Feelings > Actions > Results

7. Stories give you permission to do one of three things—defer your story, destroy your story, or design your story.

8. You have five choices of guru clans to join—the practicals, the synthesizers, the nonconformists, the academics, and the celebrities.

9. The best DJs use their GPS strategically for maximum effectiveness.

10. As long as your results are better than your potential clients, in their eyes you possess incredible value and gurulike status.

11. Joining the synthesizers requires three simple steps—obtain the best content, combine it to form new truth, and broadcast your message.

12. The Influence/Income Scale demonstrates that we reward those who add the most value.

13. Sticky stories allow people to see themselves (they're relatable), free themselves (are liberating), be themselves (are authentic), and pee themselves (are memorable).

14. Check out DayJobToDreamJob.com/resources to see examples of sticky stories.

15. Your GPS needs the right space to survive and thrive.

Step Two: DESIGN Your Space

Our Experience Reflects Your Values

> Perfection is achieved, not when there is nothing more to add, but when there is nothing left to take away.
>
> Antoine de Saint-Exupéry

I opened the front door and immediately knew I was in for a surprise. At that moment, I just had no idea how big that surprise would be.

"Excuse me, could you please tell me where sparkspace is?" I felt a little odd even saying the name.

My friend had called me last week, quite ecstatic. According to him, I just HAD to check out this amazing place in downtown Columbus, Ohio.

As a rule, I enjoy visiting the city anyway. But this felt different. My friend's enthusiasm piqued my curiosity. Typically monotone, his abnormal frequency caught my attention. "Just be ready for something like a cross between Microsoft and *Charlie and the Chocolate Factory*," he said.

OK, now he had me. Talk about a paradox. I immediately called them and booked a tour with a guy named Mark.

"Sparkspace?" the helpful stranger said. "Sure . . . head down that hallway, then take a left. Hop into the elevator and go to the second floor. Trust me. You won't miss it." She explained with a twinge of energy.

Was that just a wink? I wondered. *She must know something I don't.*

With her instructions I continued on my way.

Just finding the correct building that morning took some navigational skills. I typed in 300 Macaroni at first. Who knows why? Maybe because my youngest daughter, Addison, loves macaroni and cheese. Luckily, my smartphone is smarter than me. It autocorrected the search to *Marconi*.

Before that day I had only *heard* about the Arena District. With a day job nestled safely in the suburbs, I didn't need to venture down to this cool part of town often. But even while parking, I noticed the unique characteristics of this new environment. I suppose the quick transition from asphalt to brick paved the way.

The Arena District offers a cool experience made possible by amazing restaurants (Brazilian steakhouse included), unique residential and commercial spaces, movie theaters, indoor and outdoor concerts, and Nationwide Arena.[1]

According to the address, sparkspace appeared to be smack-dab in the middle of the district. While walking down the hallway on my way to the elevator, I noticed the beautiful contrast of original stone walls butting up to aged wood floors. Evidently, this renovated paint factory was built in the 1890s. Whoever decorated this particular walkway decided to leave some of the relics behind as accent pieces.

After locating the elevator, I entered and pressed the appropriate button for the second floor. In the fifteen-second ride up, a variety of thoughts entered my brain. Especially ones surrounding *Charlie and the Chocolate Factory.* Didn't he ride some glass elevator that transported him to another world?

Suddenly the door opened, followed by my mouth. "WOW!" I gasped.

"Hi, you must be Kary." A voice cut through my daze. It belonged to a vibrant brunette who stood behind a lime green counter.

"Umm . . . yeah . . . hi," I said.

"We get that a lot," she stated, referencing my impulsive WOW. "The whole atmosphere just kind of reaches out and grabs you, doesn't it?"

"I'll say," I responded.

"My name is Leah and I'm director of guest happiness here at sparkspace," she informed me. "Welcome to the most inspirational business retreat center on the planet."

My brain attempted to categorize what I saw, but I quickly realized the futility of my efforts. Sparkspace dominated a category all its own.

Meet Mr. Potato Head

An impressive wall of Mr. and Mrs. Potato Heads towered in front of me. The track lighting displayed these toy vegetables in all their glory. Someone had placed a sign next to them. It read:

> Have fun and
> be creative
> with our famous
> Potato Heads!
>
> What are you going to be today?

Great question, I thought to myself. *Do they want guests to play with these toys during their meetings? Interesting . . .*

The bright colors on the walls interrupted my thoughts. (I had been sure these fluorescent hues disappeared along with the Punky Brewster sitcom back in the mid-1980s. Guess I was wrong.)

As I turned to my left, a wall of candy boldly confronted me. "What's that?" I gestured.

"Oh, that's our wall of candy," she explained.

"Of course," I said, chuckling. "Pretty self-explanatory."

Then something even stranger popped into my awareness.

Personal growth books

Leadership books

Business books

"Wow," I said. Not intending to speak aloud *again*. (I imagined this "director of guest happiness" must have thought I was weird. Then again, she was the one with the weird job title.)

"What's with the book choices?" I questioned. "Most of those are my favorites."

"Oh those ones . . . those are a few of Mark's favorites too. He values learning and leadership. Wait just one moment and I'll let him know you're here."

Too immersed in my surroundings, I didn't notice her departure. Rotating 360 degrees, I observed vibrantly colored hubcaps covering an entire wall. And in another corner, I located a "wire tree" with business cards attached to the end of each "branch."

An unassuming voice cut in. "Welcome, Kary. I'm Mark . . . the chief imagination officer here at sparkspace."

I thought you were Willy Wonka.

If first impressions weren't so important I might have blurted it out loud. But thankfully I muzzled my mouth and kept my comment in my head.

"Quite a place you have here, Mark. I'm a huge fan already," I said.

"You haven't seen anything yet. Let me show you around."

And so began our tour and our subsequent friendship. Before the tour ended I wrote him a check. Motivated to secure one of his remaining sponsorship slots for an upcoming leadership event, I wanted to be identified with his space. Even after just a brief introduction, I already knew we shared many of the same values:

Creativity

Leadership

Experimentation

Growth

Expression

Risk

Freedom

Entrepreneurship

You might wonder how a sixty-minute tour of sparkspace could communicate values clearly enough for me to not only observe personally but also invest in financially.

All the credit goes to Mark and his team.

DJs Showcase Their Space

Here's what I know about space—intentionally designed space creates an experience that reflects your values.

Space is *that* powerful. But similar to the quality of your stories in the last chapter, not all spaces are created equal. For most businesses this includes virtual spaces via websites and social media. For other businesses this may also include physical spaces via buildings or stores.

Notice, space eclipses both websites and buildings. It includes but is not limited to:

Vocabulary	Inflection	Entertainment
Clothing	Process	Recreation
Titles	Frequency	Humor
Symbols	Pricing	Religion
Music	Paperwork	Sexuality
Smell	Technology	Presentation
Fashion	Policies	Topic
Style	Benefits	Art
Lighting	Aesthetics	Health
Tone	Ideology	Boundaries
Texture	Finances	What's included
Imagery	Education	What's left out

The Space Circle—A Proven Success Story

In this second step of The Dream Jobber Plan, designing your space, I could provide all kinds of theory, suggestions, and tips. This might be helpful.

Or I could show you how Mark designed sparkspace, a proven success story. Then I could extract practical steps and put them into a powerful model I call the Space Circle.

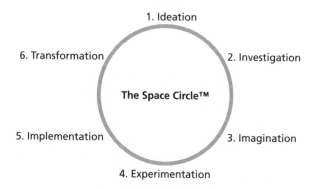

Since the latter is better, let's go with it. I'll retell the sparkspace story from Mark's perspective, drawing from our interviews. Through the process you'll realize how these six steps can help you intentionally design your space too. Doing so will allow you to create a unique experience that reflects your values.

The Space Circle

1. **Ideation**—create new ideas
2. **Investigation**—explore existing models
3. **Imagination**—form mental images
4. **Experimentation**—practice new applications
5 **Implementation**—execute the plan
6. **Transformation**—expand your awareness

1. Ideation—Create New Ideas

From Mark Henson's own perspective . . .

I started out at as a disc jockey and although I loved the job, I hated the industry. Because of this, I eventually switched to a design firm called Fitch and served as a glorified copywriter.

When clients came to our location in Worthington something peculiar took place. They left their normal offices to meet with us in this cool little space surrounded by forests and nature.

When they entered this unique space space, something changed. Or better said, something *in them* changed. At first they commented on the unique environment that fostered imagination and creativity. But those comments quickly transitioned into behavioral changes. Through our meetings their energy level and productivity increased. Over the course of the project, I saw something inside them unlock. It seemed like they experienced a new sense of freedom and innovation.

I thought about this idea for quite some time. What was it about this space that sparked this transformation?

From a young age, I always enjoyed designing spaces. I think I got it from my mom. She could easily have been an interior decorator. And she always supported my desire to design. Although I had a little 7 x 10 room, I swear I changed that design every two weeks.

As an adult, I knew most of my friends worked corporate jobs and commented on how boring their meetings felt. I knew their plain office space contributed to the problem. Columbus didn't offer any type of creative meeting spaces to help businesses step outside the status quo.

Although a potent idea pregnant with potential, my day job took precedence and I put this one on the back burner.

Takeaways:

Pay attention to what you pay attention to.

Identify your interests, talents, and unique characteristics that defined you from an early age.

Designing the right space is more about recovering where you've been than discovering where you need to go.[2]

2. Investigation—Explore Existing Models

To a fault, I'm a guy with a thousand ideas. But for some reason this one kept coming back to me. I remember attending a conference where I heard a woman from Austin, Texas, talk about the pros and cons of corporate creative spaces. Yet after a few years of running her own creative space business, she grew tired of playing "party hostess."

I sat there stunned. Here it was again, the same idea, but now from another source. And unlike the Texan's negativity, I LOVED playing party host. I was hardwired for hospitality and I enjoyed taking care of people, whether waiting tables or serving as a tour guide in Oklahoma City at the museum for free enterprise.

After a little more investigation I learned about some other cities that designed similar corporate creative spaces. Places like Eureka! Ranch, often referred to as "a safe haven for original thinking."[3]

I left the experience excited about other models that existed. In one moment, it suddenly became more possible. I committed to talk with my employer about this one idea I couldn't shake.

Takeaways:

Pinpoint a few ideas that keep coming back to you.

Explore similar models of people already doing it.

List how your idea is similar to and different from the existing models.

3. Imagination—Form Mental Images

Surprisingly, Fitch communicated tremendous support for my idea. They said they had a vision for designing a similar space. Other projects weighed heavy at the moment so they didn't have bandwidth to invest in the idea. They told me to check back with them in a few months.

I felt rejuvenated by the conversation. Since I'm a go-getter I started looking for potential spaces immediately. At the same time, I kept investing in my day job both on and off the clock. I organized both the staff picnic and the sand volleyball tournament. I wanted Fitch to recognize my value for increasing productivity and building company culture.

I also started a secret wish list for everything I'd need in the future. Fluorescent lights didn't make the list. As a kid I had a kidney problem and spent a bunch of time in hospitals. They always had fluorescent lights and I despised them.

Although I lacked a physical space for my idea, I still created an incredibly clear mental one. I knew my time would eventually come.

Takeaways:

Don't let anyone talk you out of your idea.

Make yourself valuable in your current day job.

Design your space before you have the chance to build it.

4. Experimentation—Practice New Applications

My opportunity came much sooner than expected. A nine-hundred-square-foot space in the Short North opened up almost overnight. Although the size and location weren't ideal, the vacancy motivated me to revisit the conversation with Fitch. I felt I owed them first dibs since they supported the initial idea.

They declined a partnership because the timing conflicted with their deadlines. Nonetheless, sensing my unwavering passion, they blessed my efforts.

On January 1, 2000, I opened up the new location. I called it *sparkspace* from day one knowing I wanted an incredibly clear purpose. Besides, the idea came to me in the shower and who can argue with that type of epiphany?

This single room also had a small kitchenette and a single bathroom. I loved some elements about the space:

> High ceilings
> Loft space
> Brick walls

I hated other elements about the space:

> Hookers in the alley
> Bums on the sidewalk
> An occasional robbery down the street

Even then, I knew *sparkspace* would start there, but not end there. I felt some misalignment with the space, but I'd eventually design a space that reflected all my values.

Financially, I needed to keep my day job. This meant setting up the meeting space before work. With Fitch's permission I then ran back during lunch to reset the space for the next meeting. And finally at the end of my day job, I cleaned up.

I invested the most time cleaning the restroom. (Every meeting space needs a clean restroom.) Although not ideal for business meetings, this restroom had a bathtub. Committed to improvising, I mixed things up by adding a shower curtain. And knowing people would peek behind the curtain, I placed a life-size cardboard cutout of Austin Powers in the shower.

While setting up the space, I occasionally heard a scream come from the bathroom. I couldn't help but laugh.

Someone had just met Austin.

From the beginning I injected my values into the experience. Rather than creative chaos, I chose intentional energy. Word of *sparkspace* grew slowly, but steadily. I marketed strictly to the business community and avoided birthday parties, baby showers, and social groups. I knew my target audience and always kept it front and center.

With a new baby at home, something had to give. Knowing our benefits came from my wife's job, I went back to Fitch and asked them if I could cut back my hours and compensation. They agreed and let me go to thirty hours a week.

Sparkspace continued to grow and a few months later I asked to go down to twenty hours. Again they agreed.

I believe our arrangement functioned as a win-win for both of us. A win for me because I lacked the income stream to leave suddenly. Fitch gave me a gift by allowing me to scale back my hours. A win for them because I sincerely hustled at my day job. They benefited from another year of me investing in the company.

But then the day came.

Fitch obtained a new project and needed me to increase my hours. If I couldn't go back to full-time then I needed to make a clean break.

You guessed it. We parted on good terms. They even threw me a going away party. Because of my increased clarity, I had no other choice. Truth be told, I didn't want another choice.

I left my day job and entered my dream job, forever.

Takeaways:

Ideal space comes over time. Get started now. Tweak as you go.

Hustle at all times, especially in the beginning.

Don't wait to inject your values into the experience.

If possible, engage your employer in the process. They might surprise you because they don't want to lose you.

Prepare now for the final break later.

5. Implementation—Execute the Plan

Shortly after, I relocated to the Arena District on Marconi Boulevard. Jumping into my dream job full-time afforded me the time to design the space with even more intentionality. The building contractor and I worked together to come up with ideas for the floor plan and materials.

Over the last dozen plus years we expanded to 7,500 square feet. This included a kitchen, a gallery, and five different meeting spaces. Each room has a unique name and feel:

> the loft (65 feet of windows + original art)
> the retro room (blast to the past + cushy furniture)
> the zenergy room (imagine peaceful energy)
> the think tank (colorful + ancient relics)
> the board room (outfitted with surfboards and skateboards)

But even more than the physical space, we executed a plan to design an intentional experience. We integrated our values even within our programming, marketing, and pricing.

Programming—From the beginning, our programming always developed people. Yet over the years our topics shifted. We've evolved from brainstorming, to team development, to leadership development, to customer service, to self-leadership.

Looking back, I've noticed the topics changed in relationship with my own transformation. I focused on content I needed to master in my own life. Preparing for the programs helped prepare me personally.[4]

Marketing—Any time business slows down we increase our free content. *Sparkspace* is about much more than renting space. We value personal development for business professionals. By demonstrating generosity to others and giving first, we always receive more in the end.

Pricing—We designed our rates to reflect our values. As you may have noticed, most conference centers, hotel meeting rooms, and retreat center facilities charge a much smaller fee for a meeting room than we do. Unfortunately, they also charge big money for every extra item you request. The final bill is often a shocker.

We have a better way. We include everything.

Sparkspace is the only business meeting space with all-inclusive pricing. Need an LCD projector? It's included. Need flip charts? Included. How about the little stuff like pens, notepads, markers, etc.? All included. We happily include nearly fifty items that most places charge for. And we don't charge a dime (or even a nickel) more. And you'll know exactly how much your meeting will cost up front.

How do we compare?

Here's an example of a meeting for fifteen participants based on actual pricing our clients have paid at hotels and typical conference centers.

Item	Sparkspace	Other Spaces
Meeting room	$85 per person	$350
Digital projector	FREE	$500
Projector screen	FREE	$100
Bose computer speakers	FREE	$25
Remote "clicker"	FREE	$50
DVD/VCR player	FREE	$50
WIFI/internet	FREE	$150
Flip charts	FREE	$80
Notepads	FREE	$40
Conference phone	FREE	$50
Copies	FREE	$1 per page
Faxes	FREE	$1 per fax
Beverages	FREE	$100
Light snacks	FREE	$150
Stereo	FREE	$75
Computer	FREE	$350
Pens & markers	FREE	$20
Sticky notes	FREE	$20
Room setup	FREE	$75
Extra hours	FREE	$100/hr
TOTAL	$1275	$2185 +

And here's the stuff you can only get at sparkspace:

Item	Sparkspace	Other Spaces
Digital camera	FREE	n/a
XM Radio	FREE	n/a
Ninetendo Wii	FREE	n/a
Bowls of candy	FREE	n/a
Adjustable lights	FREE	n/a
Apple adapters	FREE	n/a
Phone chargers	FREE	n/a
Games, fiddle toys	FREE	n/a
Crazy hats	FREE	n/a
Inspirational library	FREE	n/a
Concierge service	FREE	n/a
Controllable A/C	FREE	n/a
Portable whiteboard	FREE	n/a
Creative environment	FREE	really, really n/a

Who says we can't differentiate ourselves? Remember, it's our space and we get to design the experience. We intentionally integrate our personal values throughout everything we do.

Our space certainly doesn't resonate with everyone. Some naysayers tell us we're just a playground. Fine. I'll accept the *playground* part, but I'd add that we're a playground with a purpose.

At the same time, other people love us.

I'm OK either way. And I don't change who we are because some people are upset. We need to execute the plan because frankly, it's our plan.

Takeaways:

Switching to your dream job opens up opportunities and creates the time to design with more intentionality.

Focus on content that you need to master in your own life.

Incorporate generosity first into your personal character and second into your business model.

Design your pricing and compensation around your values and the unique experience you offer.

Research your competitors' pricing and space.

Differentiate yourself from your competitors and commit to delivering more value.

Don't apologize for your values.

Execute your plan realizing you'll upset some clients.

6. Transformation—Expand Your Awareness

We've come a long way from Austin Powers standing in the shower. And we've experienced our own transformation along the way.

We started *sparkspace* offering 10 percent healthy snacks and 90 percent junk food as part of our "all-inclusive light snacks." We loaded people up with candy, chips, and pop (or *soda* as they call it in some parts of the country).

Since then we've redesigned that part of our space. The experience didn't reflect our values. Here we were conducting personal growth programs on how to be high performers and then leading attendees into carb crashes and sugar rushes.

If we want to help people develop as leaders, we need to help them fight fatigue. We now offer 10 percent junk food (the candy wall still stands tall) and 90 percent healthy snacks. We offer vitamin water, gluten-free snacks, Zone Perfect bars, and other products developed by Abbot Nutrition.

Our clientele transformed too. A partial list includes:

Abercrombie & Fitch
Nationwide Insurance
Nationwide Children's Hospital
The Limited
Bath & Body Works
DSW Designer Shoe Warehouse
Grange Insurance
State Farm
JP Morgan Chase
Ohio University
The Ohio State University

We host around seven hundred meetings annually. And we've been featured in a number of publications including *Inc. Magazine*, *The Metropreneur*, and *Columbus CEO Magazine*.

Despite some of the recent accolades, our original purpose never changed. We're still committed to be *the most inspirational business retreat center on the planet*.

Since we're a retreat center we often don't see the long-term transformation. We don't mind. Clients email us all the time with incredible testimonials. They tell us how their meeting at *sparkspace* ignited the initial fire for a company-wide transformation.

That's always been our hope—create space for the initial spark.

Takeaways:

When your space is out of alignment with your values, make a shift.

Model your own transformation to your clients.

Don't compromise your purpose when success comes.

Celebrate testimonials of transformation.

Key Points

(If you RT, use #DJtoDJ to join the conversation with other DJs)

1. Intentionally designed space creates an experience that reflects your values.

2. You must position your GPS (story) within an intentionally designed space that reflects your values.

3. The Space Circle (Ideation, Investigation, Imagination, Experimentation, Implementation, Transformation) model will help you when designing your own space.

4. Designing the right space is more about recovering where you've been than discovering where you need to go.

5. Make yourself valuable in your current day job.

6. Design your space before you have the chance to build it.

7. If possible, engage your employer in the process. They might surprise you because they don't want to lose you.

8. Prepare now for the final break later.

9. Switching to your dream job opens up opportunities and creates the time to design with more intentionality.

10. Focus on content you need to master in your own life.

11. Incorporate generosity first into your personal character and second into your business model.

12. Don't apologize for your values.

13. Execute your plan realizing you'll upset some clients.

14. When your space is out of alignment with your values, make a shift.

15. Don't compromise your purpose when success comes.

Step Three:
DESIGN Your Service

Choose Your Solution,
Then Your Service Style

> You're the CEO of a company called YOU.
>
> Chet Scott

waited until this chapter for a reason. At this point in our conversation you might be asking one BIG important question:
Who is The Dream Jobber Plan for?

Businesses owners?

Entrepreneurs?

Micro-business owners?

Independent contractors?

Mobilepreneurs?

Sole proprietors?

Solopreneurs?

Employers?

Employees?

Me?

I understand the question. And I'll provide a clear answer, but first let's unpack the story behind the question.

Initially, when sharing this content, I heard people give seemingly logical reasons why they didn't need The Dream Jobber Plan. Reasons such as:

My dream job still keeps me in an employee role.

I want to work in a Fortune 500 company.

I want to work behind the scenes, not out in front.

I don't want to be my own boss.

I don't want to mess with technology.

I don't need to change.

Great reasons. Except each one of them misses the point. Even worse, each one ignores the new world in which you live.

You have a choice:

Live Ignorantly = Irrelevance and Illusion of Control

Live Enlightened = Relevance and Loss of Control

Your choice brings a cost and a reward. And I've seen these costs and rewards play out in real time throughout environments of various sizes and shapes (businesses, families, marriages, nonprofits, churches, schools, and individuals). As a student of change and transformation, here are two of my favorite quotes on the topic:

> In times of change learners inherit the earth; while the learned find themselves beautifully equipped to deal with a world that no longer exists.
>
> Eric Hoffer[1]

> If you don't like change, you're going to like irrelevance even less.
>
> Gen. Eric Shinseki, retired Chief of Staff, US Army[2]

It's your choice—ignorance or enlightenment. What's it going to be?

The Brand Called You

When the 1997 August/September issue of *Fast Company* landed in stands it rocked the business world. Revolutionary for its time, the article sounded the alarm about the changing landscape. Even the title—"The Brand Called You"—challenged current thinking.

In the article, author Tom Peters communicated some shocking sound bytes. Many still ring true today.

> To be in business today, our most important job is to be head marketer for the brand called You.
>
> Anyone can have a website. The sites you go back to are the sites you trust. The brand is a promise of the value you'll receive.
>
> When everybody has email . . . how do you decide whose messages you're going to read and respond to first—and whose you're going to send to the trash unread? The answer: personal branding. It's a promise of the value you'll receive for the time you spend reading the message.
>
> What do I do that adds remarkable, measurable, distinguished, distinctive value?
>
> What do I want to be famous for?
>
> When you're promoting brand You, everything you do—and everything you choose not to do—communicates the value and character of the brand.
>
> One key to growing your power is to recognize the simple fact that we now live in a project world. Almost all work today is organized into bite-sized packets called projects.
>
> Being CEO of Me Inc. requires you to act selfishly—to grow yourself, to promote yourself, to get the market to reward yourself.
>
> Instead of making yourself a slave to the concept of a career ladder, reinvent yourself on a semi-regular basis.
>
> You are a brand. You are in charge of your brand.[3]

It's easy to forget what life was like in 1997, and if you do the article loses some of its prophetic voice.

Remember 1997? A world with no Facebook, LinkedIn, or Twitter. Many of us still listened to music on cassette tapes. And we made calls "on-the-go" using pay phones.

Keeping it real, look how the trendy author wrote his bio at the end of the article:

Tom Peters (TJPET@aol.com) is the world's leading brand when it comes to writing, speaking, or thinking about the new economy. He has just released a CD-ROM, "Tom Peters's Career Survival Guide" (Houghton Mifflin interactive).[4]

Evidently, an AOL email address and a CD-ROM screamed "cutting edge" back then. Peters even references "beeper numbers" in the article. (Millennials, you might need to Google that word if you want to know the ancient gadget he's referring to.)

But don't let his concluding bio fool you.

Peters's 3,800 words reek with the scent of time travel. It's almost as if he hijacked a spaceship, flew into the future, peeked over the horizon, and then scribbled down what he saw.

His article's subtitle only has one phrase wrong for today's marketplace (italics mine):

Big Companies Understand the Importance of Brands.
    Today in the Age of the Individual, you *have to be* your own Brand.
    Here's what it takes to be the CEO of ME Inc.[5]

Today you no longer get the option of *having to be* your own brand. In our digitally connected world, like it or not, you *are* your own brand. And thanks to social media, your brand receives regular promotion via status updates, tweets, and tags. The only remaining question is: What kind of brand are you communicating?

Everybody can watch you everywhere, especially those with a vested interest such as prospective clients, vendors, partners, and employers. According to Gen Y expert Dan Schawbel, "A new survey . . . shows that 92 percent of employers are using or planning to use social networks for recruiting this year."[6]

His article "How Recruiters Use Social Networks to Make Hiring Decisions Now," featured in *Time* magazine, explains "What you post or Tweet can have positive or negative impact on what recruiters think of you."[7] In other words, caution: your tweets may eat your opportunities.

Schawbel isn't alone in his thinking. According to CareerBuilder.com,

Hiring managers are using social media to evaluate candidates' character and personality outside the confines of the traditional interview process. When asked why they use social networks to conduct background research, hiring managers stated the following:

> 65 percent—To see if the candidate presents himself/herself professionally.
> 51 percent—To see if the candidate is a good fit for the company culture.
> 45 percent—To learn more about the candidate's qualifications.
> 35 percent—To see if the candidate is well-rounded.
> 12 percent—To look for reasons not to hire the candidate.

A double-edged sword, social media hurts candidates just as much as it helps. Smart employers "research" their future hires as a means of managing damage control.

A third of hiring managers who currently research candidates via social media said they have found information that has caused them not to hire a candidate. That content ranges from evidence of inappropriate behavior to information that contradicted their listed qualifications:

> 49 percent—Candidate posted provocative/inappropriate photos/info.
> 45 percent—There was info about candidate drinking or using drugs.
> 35 percent—Candidate had poor communication skills.
> 33 percent—Candidate bad-mouthed previous employer.
> 28 percent—Candidate made discriminatory comments related to race, gender, religion, etc.
> 22 percent—Candidate lied about qualifications.[8]

Not in the job hunt? Think because you're employed you're now immune?

Think again!

Huffington Post published a brief article titled, "Fired Over Facebook: 13 Posts That Got People CANNED." A simple post on Facebook meant no more jobs for thirteen individuals.

The authors intro the article by explaining the purpose of social media. "Facebook's mission is to make the world a 'more open and connected' place. But the site's users can sometimes be a bit too open, posting pictures, opinions, videos, and 'jokes' via the social networking site that give employers pause—and employees the boot."[9] *Huffington* encourages readers to vote if they felt the thirteen examples of termination were excessive or deserved.

Improper photos might deserve "the axe," right? But *Huffington* also published a related article, "Fired Over Twitter: 13 Tweets That Got People CANNED," that reveals how 140 characters launched a firestorm hot enough to place some employees in the hot seat, permanently.

Toxic tweets such as:

> Cisco just offered me a job! Now I have to weigh the utility of a fatty paycheck against the daily commute to San Jose and hating the work.

According to the article, "After an interview at Cisco Systems, Connor Riley confessed in a tweet that she would hate the job but relish the 'fatty paycheck.'"[10] When a channel partner advocate for Cisco Alert stumbled across her Twitter account, Connor's fate was sealed.

Think times have changed since Tom Peter's article published in 1997? Even Pope Francis seems to think so, along with his three-million-plus Twitter followers.

Opting Out Isn't an Option

Some claim immunity by opting out of social media altogether, declaring themselves "off the grid." But even this choice communicates volumes about your personal brand. It's time to accept the truth. Every single one of us is the CEO of a company called YOU.

You might argue, "I can't afford the time or money to develop The Dream Jobber Plan." I respectfully disagree. You can't afford the time or money NOT to develop your Dream Jobber Plan.

Here's why. Regardless of your current classification . . .

Businesses owner

Entrepreneur

Micro-business owner

Independent contractor

Mobilepreneur

Sole proprietor

Solopreneur

Employer

Employee

You're still the sole manager of our own personal brand. Critics might argue they don't need:

A story

A space

A service

A platform

A product

A promotion

A community

Clarity

Credibility

Regardless of their rationale, I respectfully challenge them by pointing out:

Story—You are one. (It might not be sticky yet.)

Space—You've already designed one. (It might be ugly and unintentional.)

Service—You need a solution to help people. (Or else you're irrelevant.)

Platform—You might only have a small one. (Get noticed in a noisy world.)

Product—You need one. (Nothing to sell means no passive income.)

Promotion—You already do it. (Though it might be done poorly.)

Community—You were built for it. (No one is an island.)

Clarity—You need it. (Fogginess repels people.)

Credibility—You can't survive without it. (All relationships are built on trust.)

Functional Freelancers

I believe you should become what I call a Functional Freelancer, regardless if you're "traditionally employed." Here's a quick comparison between a Functional Freelancer and *everybody else*:

Long-Term Contractor Mindset	Functional Freelancer Mindset
Dependent posture	Self-employed posture
Blame others	Take ownership
Make excuses	Invite accountability
Embody denial	Embody responsibility
"On the clock" = waste time	"On the clock" = redeem time
Externally motivated	Internally motivated
Annual review metrics	Project review metrics
Pay based on attendance	Pay based on performance

Seeing yourself as anything other than a Functional Freelancer creates prisonlike conditions. The way you see yourself, regardless of your job title, matters. Just like Andy back in Shawshank. He may have been imprisoned on the outside, but he maintained a mindset of freedom on the inside. And as a result, Andy escaped.

When Day Jobbers adopt a Functional Freelancer Mindset, something exciting often happens. They begin to see their current employer as one large *billable client*. When Day Jobbers change the way they look at things, the things they look at change.[11]

You can fire billable clients.

You can serve billable clients.

You can respect billable clients.

With billable clients you have choices. You move from grumbling to gratitude. You begin to see the truth that imprisonment, imagined or actual, only occurs when you lose your ability to choose.

Holocaust survivor Viktor Frankl, held prisoner against his will, realized this. He wrote, "Forces beyond your control can take away everything you possess except one thing, your freedom to choose how you will respond to the situation."[12]

Head of the Class

This new mindset isn't just for employees either. I coach all my clients toward becoming Functional Freelancers. It doesn't matter if you're a CEO of a large company or a founding partner of a startup. If you see yourself improperly, you soon become imprisoned no matter how big the paycheck.

Here are three reasons why Functional Freelancers are superior.

1. They Add the Most Value

Some long-term contractors feel internally motivated and embody responsibility, but these are *the exceptions*. Remember the Gallup survey we examined? Only 3 out of 10 employees are engaged in their jobs. The remaining 70 percent are disengaged or actively disengaged. This long-term contractor mindset costs "up to $550 billion annually in lost productivity."[13]

Functional Freelancers are different. Rather than costing money, they create it. They don't receive a paycheck for showing up. They hustle to get theirs. This mindset creates people hungry for growth. Functional Freelancers realize that as they add value to themselves, they make themselves more valuable.

2. They Align with the Market

Remember John, Nancy, and Louise from chapter 1? Naturally, over time, each had adopted a long-term contractor mindset. This happened simply based upon the years they had invested in their respective companies. Although successful, each eventually appropriated a dependent posture. They found out overnight how vulnerable they actually were.

Functional Freelancers are highly aware of market trends. They know the unemployment rates, the average stay in jobs, and the fact that half of the American workforce will soon consist of *actual* freelancers.[14] This knowledge doesn't create fear. Instead, it creates the fuel to develop your own brand.

3. They Attract the Best Clients

Functional Freelancers recognize the better they become, the better clients they attract.

In his book *The 21 Irrefutable Laws of Leadership*, author John Maxwell teaches the Law of Magnetism—*who we are is who we attract.*

In the past we observed this law with the military leaders of the Civil War. Maxwell writes:

> When the Southern states seceded, there were questions about which side many of the generals would fight for. Robert E. Lee was considered the best general in the nation, and President Lincoln actually offered him command of the Union army. But Lee would never consider fighting against his native Virginia. He declined the offer and joined the Confederacy—and the best generals in the land followed him.[15]

If Lee had accepted the Union position, many historians speculate that the war would have been much shorter and hundreds of thousands of lives would have been saved. Lee was an influential leader and many of his generals would have followed him if he fought for the North.

Living in Columbus, we saw this law play out over the span of two football seasons. The Ohio State Buckeyes had an amazing 2010 season with a record of 12–1. When coach Jim Tressel resigned on May 30, 2011, his assistant coach Luke Fickell was named interim coach. Although conditions weren't ideal, Fickell coached his best and led the Buckeyes to a 6–7 season.

On November 28, 2011, Urban Meyer replaced Fickell as head coach. (Aware of Fickell's natural skill, Meyer repositioned him as co-defensive coordinator.)[16]

Some complained about the quick replacement. Others cheered. Meyer didn't care about public opinion. Instead, he went on to recruit a talented 2012 class, leading the Buckeyes to a 12-0 season. Some of the best players in the country came to OSU because of the new coach who led the team. The coach brought the players and the players brought the wins.

In business, the Functional Freelancers bring the best clients and the clients bring the wins.

What Are You Waiting For?

Some critics eventually make the shift from ignorant to enlightened. They agree with their need for The Dream Jobber Plan, but they commit another fatal flaw. They put off developing it until they feel they "need it."

If you wait to develop your plan until you jailbreak your job, then you're only shortsighted. Successfully shifting from your day job to your dream job takes strategy and momentum. The best time to develop your plan is *before* you need it.

Perhaps you have heard the old proverb about the best time to plant a tree? It's also true about developing your plan.

Question: When is the best time to develop your plan?

Answer: Eight years ago.

Question: When is the second best time?

Answer: Today.

If you're just starting on your Dream Jobber Plan, congratulations! Today is the perfect time because you're now aware you need a plan. On that point, let's take this third critical step together—*Design Your Service*.

The Service Sweet Spot

Because most people only care about the solution you offer, the best strategy for building your brand isn't focusing on yourself but on others.

When you change your focus, you soon realize people have problems
and they're asking questions:

How do I . . .

make it go faster?
make it go slower?
fix it?
break it?
build one?
feed it?
cut it?
attach it?
make it grow?
make it shrink?

How can I . . .

have more joy?
laugh more?
overcome boredom?
get a date?
get better grades?
get stronger?
lose more weight?

Although each question is different, all represent an obstacle. I call
these snags. A snag is simply:

A difficulty
A disadvantage
A hidden obstacle
An impediment

The world wants help fixing their snags. By offering an excellent
solution and then choosing the right service style, you're in business.

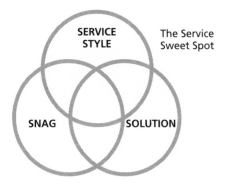

Here's what I mean.

1. Pick a Snag

Don't pick *just any* snag. Keep these three components in mind:

Pick based on awareness: DJs realize the fact they even saw a snag indicated a deeper meaning. Your awareness isn't by accident.

Pick based on interest: Bob Moore says, "Make your vocation your vacation."[17] What's an activity that doesn't seem like work for you? Why not tie that to the service you offer?

Pick based on expertise: Usually, you enjoy what you're good at. The public values competence and expertise.

2. Offer a Solution

DJs, the ones who turn their passion into their full-time gigs, make an important discovery early on in the process. They realize most people don't pay them for their hobby itself. According to Chris Guillebeau, author of *The $100 Startup*, "You get paid for helping other people pursue the hobby or for something indirectly related to it."[18]

Great solutions help people overcome their snag. We typically buy solutions, not services. Your service is merely the venue that contains your solution.

Solutions don't need to be complex. The best ones are as simple as ABC:

A—*Achievable*

Make sure it works. Test it. Provide results. Include testimonials.

B—*Believable*

Provide a guarantee—even better, provide a risk reversal guarantee. Marketing genius Jay Abraham explains the principle behind the promise. First, identify the various reasons a potential customer would hesitate to buy. Second, think of how to overcome those obstacles by transferring the risk of the purchase from the buyer to the seller.[19]

Here's a quick summary of guarantees below. Thinking as a buyer, which one do you enjoy receiving the best? Thinking as a seller, which one should you offer?

LEVEL 1—THE STANDARD GUARANTEE

Buyers receive a thirty-day period (sometimes less) to return the product for a full refund. Example: Best Buy. The standard guarantee lingo:

Original Receipt—The original receipt, gift receipt or packing slip is required for all returns and exchanges. If returning or exchanging an item in a Best Buy store, a valid photo ID is also required.
Return and Exchange Period:

15 days for all eligible products
60 days for eligible products for Reward Zone Premier members
Best Buy reserves the right to deny any return or exchange.[20]

LEVEL 2—THE EXTENDED TIME PERIOD GUARANTEE

Buyers receive a full ninety days to try the product. Example: Lowe's. The extended time period guarantee lingo:

Lowe's—Customer satisfaction is our goal. If you are not completely satisfied with your purchase, simply return the merchandise to any

Lowe's store in the United States within 90* days. We, in our discretion, will repair it, replace it, or, based on your method of payment with a valid receipt, refund your money.[21]

Level 3—The Risk Reversal Guarantee

Sellers assume the risk of the purchase, providing buyers peace of mind and 100 percent satisfaction. Example: Zappos Shoes. The risk reversal guarantee lingo:

> *FREE Shipping*: Unlike many other websites that have special rules and lots of fine print, Zappos.com offers free shipping on all domestic orders placed on our website, with no minimum order sizes or special exceptions.
>
> *FREE Returns*: If you are not 100 percent satisfied with your purchase, you can return your order to the warehouse for a full refund. (Returns must be unworn, in the state you received them, and in the original packaging.) We believe that in order to have the best possible online shopping experience, our customers should not have to pay for domestic return shipping.
>
> With Zappos Retail, Inc.'s 365 day return policy, there are no special catches or exceptions. All we ask is that you send the items back to us in the original packaging, and make sure that the merchandise is in the same condition.
>
> You can return your purchase for up to 365 days from the purchase date. If you purchase on 2/29 of a Leap Year, then you have until 2/29 the following Leap Year to return those orders. That's four whole years! Woot![22]

C—Conceivable

Make sure your solution is easily understandable. Break it down into bite-sized chunks. Remove noise, clutter, and confusing "insider" language.

3. Choose a Service Style

True, some people receive compensation purely based on the products they create. But many receive compensation for their services too.

I've found this to be true in my own DJ journey. If I relied purely on book sales, my business would struggle. Instead, I have created multiple streams of income based on a service/product combination.

For some industries, this requires a change in traditional thinking. But try. Remember, you shouldn't see yourself as a cog in the big giant machine. You should see yourself as a Functional Freelancer. Don't view yourself for what you currently do but rather for who you can become.

Remember our friend Tom Peters, the "Brand Called You" boy? He exhorted us even back in 1997, "You don't 'belong to' any company for life, and your chief affiliation isn't to any particular 'function.' You're not defined by your job title and you're not confined by your job description."[23]

Serve in Your Own Style

With that in mind, it's time for you to choose your service style. I've included a partial sampling below. Many more options exist, but this will help you get started:

Service Styles

Teaching—sharing information
Training—sharing skills
Mentoring—sharing experience
Consulting—sharing advice
Tutoring—sharing guidance
Creating—sharing inspiration
Specializing—sharing expertise
Speaking—sharing content
Writing—sharing stories
Counseling—sharing therapy
Coaching—sharing transformation

In Dream Job Bootcamp I help clients develop their Service Sweet Spot. This process includes identifying their service style too. We don't have the time to explain every distinction between these service styles. However, here's one simple difference between counseling and coaching.

> Counseling is moving someone from dysfunctionality (in a certain area) to functionality.
>
> Coaching is moving someone from functionality to potentiality.

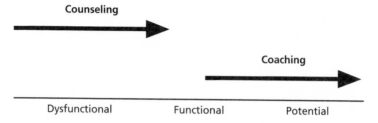

By picking a snag, offering a solution, and then choosing a service style, you've designed your Service Sweet Spot. This awareness allows you to serve people better and faster.

Quite naturally, it also produces a pretty cool byproduct too. Expanding your personal brand—the brand called YOU.

Key Points

(If you RT, use #DJtoDJ to join the conversation with other DJs)

1. You have a choice to live ignorantly or to live enlightened. Each one brings a cost and a reward.

2. Today you no longer get the option of *having to be* your own brand. In the digitally connected world, like it or not, you *are* your own brand.

3. You can't afford the time or money NOT to develop your Dream Jobber Plan.

4. You should become a Functional Freelancer, regardless if you're "traditionally employed."

5. A title means little. A mindset means much more.

6. Imprisonment occurs, imagined or actual, when you lose your option to choose.

7. If you see yourself improperly, you soon become imprisoned, no matter how big the paycheck.

8. Functional Freelancers realize that as they add value to themselves, they make themselves more valuable.

9. Functional Freelancers recognize that the better they become, the better the clients they attract.

10. If you wait to develop your plan until you want to jailbreak your job, then you're only shortsighted.

11. People care about the solution you offer.

12. Three steps make up the Service Sweet Spot—Pick a Snag, Offer a Solution, and Choose a Service Style.

13. Great solutions are achievable, believable, and conceivable.

14. Consider implementing a risk reversal guarantee within your service where you, the seller, assume the risk of the purchase.

15. The byproduct of designing your Sweet Spot Service is that you also expand your own personal brand.

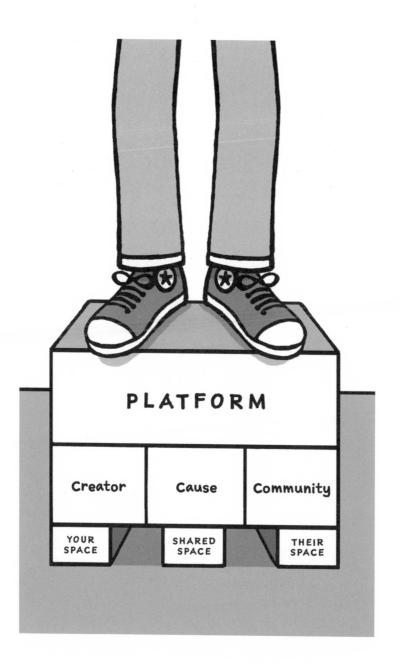

Step Four:
CREATE Your Platform

If You Want to Be Heard, You Must Be Seen

Great ideas are no longer enough. Without a platform—something that enables you to get seen and heard—you don't have a chance.

Michael Hyatt

The violin he used cost 3.5 million dollars. Handcrafted in 1713 by Antonio Stradivari, it had been stolen twice throughout its three-hundred-year life. Stradivari is thought to have made his varnish "from an ingeniously balanced cocktail of honey, egg whites and gum arabic from sub-Saharan trees."[1]

On a January morning, a musical genius stood in a metro station in Washington, DC, and started to play the violin. According to his article in the *Washington Post*, staff writer Gene Weingarten reported that the violinist's first piece, "Chaconne" by Bach, is "not just one of the greatest pieces of music ever written, but one of the greatest achievements of any man in history. It's a spiritually powerful piece, emotionally powerful, structurally perfect."[2]

This violinist played six pieces, in total about forty-five minutes.

Because of rush hour, over one thousand people went through the station, most of them on their way to work.

After the first three minutes went by, a middle-aged man noticed the musician playing. He slowed his pace, stopped for a few seconds, and then hurried off to work.

A minute later, the violinist received his first dollar tip: a woman placed her money down and continued to walk without stopping.

A few minutes later, someone leaned against the wall to listen to him, but the man looked at his watch and started to walk again. Clearly his work called him away.

The one who paid the most attention was a three-year-old boy. His mother pulled him along, but the child stopped to look at the violinist. Finally the mother pushed hard, blocking his line of sight as they walked away. Persistently, the child fought for a glimpse, but without success. This action was repeated by several other children. All the parents, without exception, forced them to move on.

In the forty-five minutes the musician played, only seven people stopped and stayed for at least one minute. Twenty-seven people gave him money but continued to walk their normal pace. He collected thirty-two dollars. (Typically his talents command a thousand dollars a minute, not seventy-one cents.) When he finished playing and silence took over, no one noticed it. No one applauded.

Only one woman recognized the identity of the violinist playing that morning—Joshua Bell, one of the best musicians in the world. "Three days before his subway station performance, Bell played to a full house at Boston's stately Symphony Hall, where average seats went for $100. Two weeks later, at the Music Center at Strathmore, in North Bethesda, he would play to a standing-room-only audience so respectful of his artistry that they stifled their coughs until the silence between movements."[3]

The *Washington Post* organized this "incognito concert" as part of a social experiment about perception, taste, and priorities of people. The questions that flowed from the experiment are rich, just like the musical talent which performed it:

Do you perceive beauty?

Do you stop to appreciate it?

Do you recognize the talent in an unexpected context?

Within the context of Step Four in The Dream Jobber Plan (Create Your Platform), the parallels are painfully telling. There's no better story that illustrates your desperate need for a platform.

Joshua Bell's talent didn't change that cold January morning. He didn't hold back or skimp for his unappreciative audience. Despite his best attempts, no one heard his music, because no one even saw his talent.

He lacked one thing—a platform.

Without a Platform You Won't Stand

In the past, you simply needed a great product. Word of mouth marketing spread the news and then your business grew.

Today, a great product is only the baseline. Without it you won't survive. But as with Joshua Bell in the crowded subway, a great product is no longer enough. You now need a platform.

According to Michael Hyatt, "Great ideas are no longer enough. Without a platform—something that enables you to get seen and heard—you don't have a chance. Having an awesome product, an outstanding service, or a compelling cause is no longer enough."[4]

In the old days, people would stand on "soapboxes" and communicate their message. These raised platforms were often wooden crates originally used for shipment of soap or other dry goods from a manufacturer to a retail store. "Soapboxes" functioned as inexpensive and portable temporary platforms for street corner speakers attempting to be seen and heard at improvised outdoor meetings. (A little less convenient than Twitter.)

Today, such "soapbox" strategies only prove ineffective and annoying. Marketers classify this as "interruption marketing." This marketing often creates ill feelings rather than good will.

Interruption Marketing? Get a Clue!

According to Seth Godin, *interruption marketing* is communicating messages that interrupt customers while they are doing something of their preference.[5] Examples include advertisements on television and radio.

Most businesses prefer interruption marketing because it's faster, easier, and cheaper. Examples include:

Purchasing email lists

Spamming (illegal)

Running ads

Placing flyers on windshields

Delivering free community papers to your door

Unfortunately, this type of marketing doesn't work in the long run. Here's why. Think of the internet as one big, noisy room. If you're on social media you already hear your friends and families friends "talking" to you regularly. They say:

LIKE this

RT that

SHARE my pic

COMMENT on my update

Although you love them, because of the sheer volume, their noise can be deafening. Besides the voices you want to hear, you also hear endless businesses shouting from their soapboxes:

SPECIAL OFFER

LIMITED TIME ONLY

BONUS INCLUDED

ACT NOW

BUY ON CREDIT

NEW AND IMPROVED

Naturally, you tune out these interruptions. Think of it as someone standing on the street corner screaming out their marriage proposals to passersby. You end up resenting those businesses.

You see right through it.

You sniff out their desire for a quick sale.

You know these businesses don't truly care about you.

Permission marketing is different. Notice the difference, also explained by Seth Godin, who literally wrote the book on the topic, *Permission Marketing.*

Permission Marketing? Get Going!

Permission marketing is the privilege (not the right) of delivering anticipated, personal and relevant messages to people who actually want to get them. Real permission is different from presumed or legalistic permission. Just because you somehow get my email address doesn't mean you have permission. Just because I don't complain doesn't mean you have permission. Just because it's in the fine print of your privacy policy doesn't mean it's permission either. Real permission works like this: if you stop showing up, people complain, they ask where you went.[6]

In today's marketplace, permission marketing works much better. Think of it as a relationship built slowly over time. This takes time and humility.

You defer your "ask" until later.

You give with no strings attached.

You care about your customers by valuing their time.

Kill the Complexity—Use the Simple Platform Plan

Today people create many excellent articles, books, and podcasts to explain the importance of building a powerful platform. With so many voices speaking, the conversation is shifting toward complexity and confusion. People weigh in with different opinions on such questions as:

What exactly is a platform?

Is my platform my tribe?

Is my tribe my platform?

Is my platform my message?

Do I build a platform and then discover my message?

An avid student of these materials, I've committed thousands of dollars and hundreds of hours studying these trends, principles, and practices. That being said, I'm also a communicator. One of my mentors, John Maxwell, arguably one of the best communicators on the planet, swears by simplicity. He distinguishes between communicators and professors:

> Communicators make complex things simple.
>
> Professors make simple things complex.[7]

Regardless if you agree or not, my goal is to make this entire book very simple, this step included. Therefore, I've created the Simple Platform Plan. If you can understand a few boxes on a page, then you're in. Like I said, simple.

I'll show the metaphor, then I'll provide examples. And once you understand it, you can create our own.

Let's begin by discovering every platform is made up of three separate parts—the posts, the planks, and the platform.

PLATFORM = ability to be seen and heard		
Creator = GPS	Cause = Idea	Community = Tribe
your space	shared space	their space

The Posts

Keeping with the Simple Platform Plan metaphor, solid platforms stand upon solid posts. And every platform has three main posts.[8]

POST ONE: YOUR SPACE

This is truly your own space. Think of it as digital space, although it might also include physical space. (For more clarity on "space" refer to Step Two—Design Your Space.)

The key here is control. You determine what gets featured, sold, listed, or published. Examples of your space include a website or blog. Here are the differences between the two:

Websites are often "one and done," simply because of their structure. You visit them once, then you're done. You might return to a website out of curiosity or the need to purchase a product. But for the most part it's static content.

Blogs (at least the good ones) publish fresh, valuable content. Because of the ability to comment, blogs often foster a sense of community too. Blogs should include the ability for readers to subscribe in exchange for providing their email address. This enables you to send your content to readers automatically.

You can start a basic blog or website with a free service like Type pad.com, Blogger.com, or Wordpress.com, for example. However, these spaces technically aren't your own space. The respective companies host it; therefore they put their company name in the address as free marketing for themselves (e.g., www.MyName.wordpress. com, www.MyName.blogspot.com).

Most people dismiss businesses, websites, and blogs like this. They figure, "If someone can't spend a few bucks a month to run their business then I don't want to buy from them." Although you might start with a free service to try it out, don't stay here. (You can switch later on. All it takes is a little time.)

Think about making your space truly your space. For around five dollars a month you can choose a self-hosted website or blog. Not only will this legitimize you, but it will also allow you to customize your space much more easily. In about twenty minutes you can set up your own self-hosted website. I use a hosting service called Bluehost. (For more free tools see DayJobToDreamJob.com/tools.)

Choose a domain name that makes sense. You can purchase this through any domain registration service, including Bluehost. This will cost you around ten dollars a year, but it will allow you to email clients from your customized email address (jon@jonsmith.com) instead of a free one (jonsmith@hotmail.com).

Although there are many opinions on what domain name to choose, if it's available I suggest choosing your own first and last name together (www.jonsmith.com). I've already purchased domain names for my children, even though they're quite young. In many cases virtual property is even more valuable than many physical properties. (Some domain names have been auctioned for millions of dollars.)

Other people purchase a domain name based upon their businesses. Simply pick something that makes sense for you and your dream job.

Post Two: Shared Space

You don't own shared space, but you can have a presence. To show up here, you must register or create a profile. Examples include:

flickr.com—a photo sharing site

pinterest.com—collect and organize things you love

gmail.com—for all Google accounts

disqus.com—a commenting platform

youtube.com—a video sharing site

twitter.com—a social network

facebook.com—a social network

linkedin.com—a professional social network

Remember this is *shared* space. Many businesses find this out the hard way. Amassing thousands of "LIKES" on Facebook doesn't mean much if you can't connect directly with your clients or fans. When these shared spaces (like Facebook) change their "rules" it can mean lost connection and lost revenue if you haven't collected individuals' email addresses.

Post Three: Their Space

These are spaces where people talk about you, your businesses, or your brand. People may feature you on their own blog, RT you on their own Twitter account, or share your posts on their own Facebook wall. You can stay in the know about such mentions through a free tool called Google Alerts.[9]

The Planks

Keeping with the Simple Platform Plan metaphor, solid platforms need solid planks to communicate effectively. Every platform has three main planks.

PLANK ONE: CREATOR/GPS

DJs knows their platforms begin and end with them. They're the creators. In the beginning, many people make the mistake of focusing on building their platforms instead of building themselves. Whatever's inside you (the good, the bad, the ugly) will be broadcasted in a bigger way when you're standing on a bigger platform.

This reality shouldn't scare you, because nobody's perfect. However, this awareness should point you in the most important direction—the mirror. If you want to grow your platform, you must grow yourself. Goethe said, "Before you can do something, you must first be something."[10]

In his book *The Rare Find: How Great Talent Stands Out*, George Anders tells an insightful story from the perspective of Bob Gibbons, a young recruiter.

> I remember the first time I saw Michael Jordan play. It was a high-school tournament in North Carolina in 1981. Jordan excelled on the court. Michael came up to me and said: "Hello, Mr. Gibbons. What did you think about my game, and what can I do to improve?" It's so rare to see that. Most players want to brag about their dunks. He didn't. He wanted to get better.[11]

You need the same commitment for your own improvement. The more you grow, the more your platform grows. Your GPS (Guru Positioning Story) communicates this growth journey in a "sticky" story people can remember and understand.

PLANK TWO: CAUSE/IDEA

Words carry weight because they inspire ideas—and ideas can change the world. We observe this in Leonardo DiCaprio's character, Cobb, from the film *Inception*. Although a fictional story, this commentary on the power of an idea is also couched in truth.

Cobb explains, "What's the most resilient parasite? *An idea*. A single idea from the human mind can build cities. An idea can transform the world and rewrite all the rules."[12]

Every healthy platform centers on a clear idea. Foggy ideas create frustrating platforms because people can't see what you stand for. Pick a fight (with an issue, not a person). Here are a few examples of businesses that picked a fight.

Business	Fight	Idea
Wal-Mart	High prices	"Save money, live better"
Ajax	Dirt	"Stronger than dirt"
Cousins Subs	Bad bread	"Better bread, better subs"
DeBeers	Temporal Mindset	"Diamonds are forever"
Nike	Excuses	"Just do it"

I coach my clients to pick their idea based on a simple acronym (I.D.E.A.S.).

I—**Integrity.** Make sure your idea is true to you, your brand, and your GPS. "FedEx—The world on time."

D—**Different.** Differentiate yourself from an overcrowded market. Unique is good. "Harley Davidson—American by birth. Rebel by choice."

E—**Effortless.** Don't force it. You want sticky, not overly clever. "Toms Shoes—Buy one, give one."

A—**Agreement.** Your idea should agree with your promise. Include a benefit. "Disney Land—The happiest place on earth."

S—**Simple.** Use proven words and short keywords. More than one word, less than seven. "Intel—Intel inside."

Your idea doesn't need to cover all five of these components. However, it should clearly address at least one.

PLANK THREE: COMMUNITY/TRIBE

Without a community, you're simply on a stage singing a solo—not too entertaining. A community changes that. They not only hear your idea, they also expand it.

Community can be a fuzzy word. I like *tribe* better because it's clearer. According to Seth Godin, "A tribe is any group of people, large or small, who are connected to one another, a leader, and an idea."[13] Based on Seth's definition, a tribe is connected to:

A leader: that's you, the creator.

An idea: that's your cause.

Each other: that's your community.

So how do you get a tribe and then build it bigger?

Although there are many different methods, DJs build their tribes strategically and intentionally. My former high school classmate Danny Gokey built his tribe by becoming the third-place finalist on season 8 of *American Idol*. More than a quarter of a million Facebook fans later, you could say his tribe grew quickly.

Since most of us won't find our tribe through a television show, we must find it another way. Again, time prevents me from explaining multiple methods. However, I'll share a quick and effective one below. I call it Three-Step Tribe Building.

1. **Be real.** Your tribe wants authenticity. Today we sniff out posers and fakes in a matter of nanoseconds. Tribes buy into you first. Hang out with them online. Be available and accessible. Build community around your blog post comments. Ask questions. *Show* genuine interest by *being* genuinely interested.

   Example: Recently, I heard a podcast titled: "What I Learned about Leadership from a Fight with My Wife."[14] I appreciated the creator's candor. We, the listeners, related to his experience because of our own fights with our own spouses. We tuned in because we were shocked someone was willing to talk about something we've all seen.

2. **Give first.** Create something worth value. Give away your best. Defer your "ask" until sometime in the future—maybe never. Write an ebook, a manifesto, or a special report. (I'll show you how in Step Nine.) Record a video, a training, or a webinar. Don't hold back. Believe in abundance, not scarcity.

> **Example:** Near my house, we're blessed with Rita's Italian Ice. I'll admit. I drove past it for years. No real reason. I just kept on driving. One day my friend told me Rita's was giving away a free Italian Ice to everyone who stopped in. Their reason? The first day of spring. I figured, why not? The kids and I stopped on our way to the park. Guess who joined the Rita's tribe now? My kids! They ask me to stop again—often. Smart people at Rita's.

3. **Get permission.** You now know the difference between interruption marketing and permission marketing. Although slower, permission is the best way to go. Interruption is mostly a waste of time and money. Get permission by using a free service such as Feedburner or MailChimp (up to a certain number of subscribers). Paid services include Aweber, Constant Contact, and iContact. Give away the free product you created above in exchange for an email address. It's clean. It's fast. And the autoresponder feature will save you time.

> **Example:** We recently created a special screencast called "Discover Your Purpose."[15] I put some of my best content in this forty-five-minute, power-packed teaching. In the first week hundreds of people signed up for this free training. This free giveaway built our tribe the best way—with people's permission.

The Platform

Michael Hyatt, the guru who literally wrote the book *Platform*, said it best—a platform is "something that gives us the ability to be seen and heard."[16]

Keeping with the Simple Platform Plan metaphor, the stronger your posts and planks, the bigger your platform. You need a strong platform because you need to be seen and heard. Your message is that important.

Thankfully, musicians like Joshua Bell have strong posts *and* strong planks. Naturally, the world sees and hears him because of his ever-expanding platform. His products gain traffic and traction because his passionate tribe feels committed to him (the creator), his cause (the idea), and his community (the rest of the tribe).

DJs know it's easier to create great products after they create strong platforms. That said, it's time to take the next step: Step Five—Create Your Product.

Key Points

(If you RT, use #DJtoDJ to join the conversation with other DJs)

1. A great product is no longer enough. You now need a platform too.

2. Without a platform—something that enables you to get seen and heard—you don't have a chance.

3. Interruption marketing rarely works and often creates ill feelings rather than goodwill.

4. "Permission marketing is the privilege (not the right) of delivering anticipated, personal and relevant messages to people who actually want to get them."[17]

5. Every platform is made up of three separate parts: the posts, the planks, and the platform itself.

6. Post one is your space. You determine what gets featured, sold, listed, or published.

7. Post two is shared space. You don't own this space, but you can have a presence.

8. Post three is their space. These are spaces where people talk about you, your businesses, or your brands.

9. Plank one is Creator/GPS. The more you grow, the more your platform grows.

10. Plank two is Cause/Idea. Every healthy platform centers on a clear idea; foggy ideas create frustrating platforms.

11. Create your clear idea using the simple acronym I.D.E.A.S. (Integrity, Different, Effortless, Agreement, Simple).

12. Plank three is Community/Tribe. Without a community you're simply on a stage singing a solo.

13. Three-step tribe building means being real, giving first, and get-
    ting permission.

14. Create something worth value, give away your best, and defer
    your ask until sometime in the future.

15. Strong platforms spread ideas.

Step Five:
CREATE Your Product

Products Increase Influence, Impact, and Income

It's all about one thing: creative problem-solving to get the story out.

Robert Greenberg

Jillian, John, and Brian are very different. Jillian loves health, John loves leadership, and Brian loves marketing. Each has a different calling and each has achieved unparalleled success. Despite their differences, each came to the same realization at different times in their careers—the more success they achieved, the less accessible they became.

When DJs reach this level of success, they have a choice. They can keep adding more activity to their plates and burn out. Or they can increase their influence, impact, and income by creating products.

Here's the difference—more activity yields active income, and more product yields passive income. Activity brings limits because of your own limitations—your finite amount of time, presence, and energy. But products are limitless because they're not dependent upon these factors.

Although creating product isn't necessary to join the DJs, passive income is. And if you want more freedom, finances, and fulfillment (the three benefits experienced by every DJ), then you need to create products.

In Step Five, we'll explore why Jillian, John, and Brian each created their own products. Then we'll look at sixteen different kinds of products and how they're different. And finally, we'll take a tool tour. This quick peek will help you create passive income by helping you create your own products.

Jillian—Products Increase Influence

Raised by her mother, from a young age Jillian Michaels suffered from a tough childhood defined by low self-image and psychological issues. Her parents' divorce didn't help.

By eighth grade she carried 175 lbs on her five-foot two-inch frame and hid in the classroom to avoid being terrorized.[1] Kids teased her about her unibrow, the size of her nose, and the fat rolling over her jeans.[2]

Martial arts became her lifeline. Through physical activity she regained control of her life. After some college and bartending, in 2002 she opened her own gym at the age of twenty-eight. Although she influenced people's health on a small scale back then, everything changed in 2005 when she took the role of personal trainer on the NBC reality television show *The Biggest Loser*.

I watched the show a time or two and I couldn't believe the transformation I saw. Not only did these contestants lose massive weight, they also experienced massive change. The episode I saw showed the contestants months later back in their "real" lives. Many continued to live out the transformation that began on the show.

Intelligently, Jillian didn't limit her influence to a popular television show. She increased it by creating products. Her own website tells the story.[3] Jillian Michaels is a bestselling author, a daytime Emmy-nominated television personality, an entrepreneur, and one of the nation's leading health and wellness experts. Every week she motivates millions in every form of media from television to publishing to the 1.6 million monthly visitors to her website and to her daily email newsletter. As a motivator and role model, Jillian has a unique connection with her audience that stems from her own personal journey toward wellness.

Her health and fitness empire includes books, DVDs, and video games. She authored several books: *Winning by Losing* (2007), *Making the Cut* (2008), *Master Your Metabolism* (2009), *The Master Your Metabolism Cookbook* (2010), and *The Master Your Metabolism Calorie Counter* (2010). She has also released a variety of workout DVDs and even a fitness-themed video game, *Jillian Michaels' Fitness Ultimatum*, available for Nintendo Wii.

Her popular weekly podcast, *The Jillian Michaels Show*, is available for free download on iTunes and was awarded the coveted iTunes Rewind award for the best new audio podcast in its first year.

Jillian has a popular iPhone app, Jillian Michaels Slim-Down Solution, available from iTunes, and also continues her partnership with ICON Health & Fitness on a line of in-home fitness equipment. Together with BodyMedia, she developed the Jillian Michaels 360° Weight Loss Navigator to be a key tool in providing accurate data tracking, tips, motivation, and other crucial information for those working to get and stay fit.

By creating products, Jillian clearly increased her influence upon the world.

John—Products Increase Impact

John C. Maxwell started his professional career as a pastor. Born with a leadership bent, he quickly grew the churches he oversaw. Early in his career John realized his impact would only extend as far as he did. Although he could impact people directly through his activities, he realized he could impact even more through products.

According to *Success* magazine, "His first book, *Think on These Things*, was released in 1979 and had 100 pages in 33 chapters. When someone approached him at a recent event and asked why he had so many chapters in the book, he admitted that's all he could think of. 'It was my first book, and for some of the chapters, one page was too many. If I didn't have anything more to say, I just went on to the next chapter.'"[4]

Despite his small beginnings in publishing. John has gone on to write more than eighty books and sell over twenty million copies. He was also one of only twenty-five authors named to Amazon. com's 10th Anniversary Hall of Fame. John left one of the fastest growing churches in America in 1995 to pursue writing and speaking full-time.

Besides his incredible success as a writer, John excels as a communicator. In 2012 he received the coveted Toastmasters International Golden Gavel Award.[5] Rather than just speaking at live events, decades ago John began putting his teachings on cassette tapes through a program called INJOY for nonprofit leaders and MIC (Maximum Impact Club) for business leaders. These teachings have impacted hundreds of thousands of leaders in multiple sectors of society.

Maxwell remains one of the most sought-after speakers by the Fortune 500 and around the globe. "When I die, I don't want to be known as the leadership guru or the greatest leader that ever lived in my generation or whatever," he says. "I want to be known as the person who trained more leaders than anyone else."[6]

No one can argue with his impact upon leaders around the world. The nonprofit he founded in 1996, EQUIP Leadership Inc., is a global leadership development organization committed to radically changing the leadership landscape. EQUIP seeks to train leaders to reach every nation around the world through live conferences, biblically centered resources, technology, and partnerships.

The purpose of EQUIP can be boiled down to one sentence: "We train one—to influence more and impact many."[7]

By creating products, John clearly increased his impact upon the world.

Brian—Products Increase Income

If you use Facebook, you've probably seen Brian Moran—or at least his ads. But this marketing genius stumbled into product creation almost by accident.

Brian graduated from college into one of the worst employment markets in US history in 2008. He managed to scramble together work and eventually found himself in a well-paying job, at least compared to his peers at that time. Unfortunately, he didn't like his job.

He played baseball in college. Always wanting to own his own business, he considered blending two passions—baseball and marketing. He stumbled across information about how to make money online and started consuming every podcast and every blog.[8] Although he didn't make a dime, his resolve didn't waver.

Brian learned a bunch about blogging, WordPress, search engine optimization, driving traffic, social media, product creation, and membership sites. Although he had knowledge, he lacked results and therefore income.

He began using Facebook fan pages to drive more traffic to his baseball website. Although he struggled with search engine optimization and Google AdWords, Facebook came easy.

With some testing and tweaking, his sales increased. His tiny list of sixty baseball players quickly turned into ten thousand Facebook fans in less than six months.

One day he met a guy also in the baseball training market who suggested he start teaching his Facebook techniques. Brian launched this new business and it quickly surpassed his baseball business.[9]

Brian eventually quit his job and now generates over $100,000 a month thanks to his online products, primarily driven by Facebook traffic.

By creating products, Brian clearly increased his income.

Different Products Create Different Outcomes

Before the internet, DJs didn't have as many options for creating products. Today we have a bit more. I've listed sixteen different products with an explanation for each. You'll see creating your own product is easier than you think.

> **Ebooks**—A book-length publication in digital form, consisting of text, images, or both, that is produced on, published through, and readable on computers or other electronic devices.

Books—A hard copy work of fiction or nonfiction.

Teleseminars—Used to provide information or training, or promote or sell products, to groups of people interested in a particular topic. Teleseminars are similar to traditional seminars, in content and purpose, but they are given over a teleconference or bridge line rather than at a specific location.[10] They can be recorded and listened to over the phone with a playback number.

Audioprograms—A digital program you listen to.

Webinars—A presentation, lecture, or workshop transmitted over the web.[11] The lecturer and attendees interact and collaborate. (Technically, this is active income since the lecturer must be physically present on the webinar.)

Webcasts—A media presentation distributed over the internet using streaming video technology to distribute a single content source to many simultaneous listeners/viewers. A webcast may either be distributed live or on-demand. Essentially, webcasting is "broadcasting" over the internet. Unlike webinars, the lecturer and attendees don't interact or collaborate. (This is true passive income.)

Continuity/Membership—Communities (physical or online) where members pay a regular subscription fee (usually monthly) for access to premium content, tools, and resources such as articles, special reports, monthly newsletters, expert interviews, members-only forums, or vendor lists. These communities can receive their content via hard or digital copy.

Online courses—Using a framework (model, system, structure, content, etc.) to educate through the use of electronic media.

DVD programs—Using a framework (model, system, structure, content, etc.) to educate through physical DVDs.

CD programs—Using a framework (model, system, structure, content, etc.) to educate through physical CDs.

Certifications—A designation earned by a person to assure qualification to perform a job or task. Certifications can occur within the context of a product (passive income).

Screencasting—A digital recording of computer screen output, also known as a video screen capture, often containing audio narration.

Below are four examples of services. Each are classified as active income because they require your physical presence the first time you do the service. However, each can be recorded and later turned into products that produce passive income.

Speeches—A form of communication in spoken language, made by a presenter before an audience for a given purpose.

Seminars—Any group or meeting for holding discussions or exchanging information.

Masterminds—Napoleon Hill said it best in his book *Think and Grow Rich*: "A mastermind is the coordination of knowledge and effort of two or more people, who work toward a definite purpose, in the spirit of harmony."[12]

Group Coaching—A small group in which there is the application of coaching principles.

Time to Create Your Product

I used to think creating a product was unbelievably difficult—until I created my first one. Now looking back, I realized the toughest part of creating my product was *the thought* of creating it. The more I thought about it, the more fear I felt.

This normal feeling is captured in something called Parkinson's Law. According to the law:

Work expands to fill the time available for its completion.[13]

The thing to be done swells in perceived importance and complexity in direct ratio with the time to be spent in its completion.[14]

Translation? The more you think about a simple task, the more complex it becomes. Your anxiety and stress will increase until the task is completed. What should take two hours ends up taking two weeks because you stew on it. This cumulative mental anguish saps up more energy than necessary.

You sidestep this law by creating your first product. And here's the catch—you need to do it within the next twenty-three hours. (Only twenty-three minutes is necessary, but I realize you might be at your day job reading this book and I don't want you getting fired. I'd rather have you complete The Dream Jobber Plan and exit strategically.)

If you have a computer or a smartphone, you have all the tools you need. Record yourself via video or audio. Share your GPS or a simple story. Then BOOM. You have your product.

Will it be bad?

Of course!

At least your first try will be bad. But don't give up. Take action. Do you want to stay in that day job prison forever? Sometimes it seems easier. But you're not one who gives up easily.

You're a DJ. Time to embrace it.

Take the Tool Tour

I didn't want to write an entire book about product development. That being said, I wanted to give you enough information to get you started. (If you want more help with your particular products, consider Dream Job Bootcamp.)

Most of the tools listed below include detailed instructions and videos on their respective websites. These will remove any apprehension you might feel. Many also include customer support too. For an extensive list of tools and tips, visit DayJobtoDreamJob.com/tools. You'll also enjoy the fact that all the tools are hyperlinked for ease of access.

As with all technology, new tools will release in the future. Don't let this stop you. Your time is now. These tools will help you create products that increase your influence, impact, and income.

One last thing before the tool tour. Even if you don't plan to create your products now, still check these tools out. Reading through the descriptions will expand your awareness. You'll realize you have tremendous support for escaping your day job and pursuing your dream job.

Now for the tool tour:

Ebooks

Kindle Direct Publishing—Publish your books independently with Kindle Direct Publishing (KDP) on the Amazon Kindle Store.

Vook—You write the book—they make the ebook. Vook publishes digital books that combine text, video, links to the internet, and social media into singular applications available both online and as mobile applications. They don't just convert manuscripts; they style and enhance ebooks to tell compelling stories that might not have been possible in print.

Self-Published Books

Westbow—a division of Thomas Nelson. They help authors self-publish books. Some titles are eventually published by the traditional publisher, Thomas Nelson.

Xulon Press—Print-on-demand self-publisher of Christian books.

Lightning Source—Provides a comprehensive suite of inventory-free on-demand print and distribution services for books to the publishing industry. Print books in any quantity and provide your customers access to the most comprehensive book channel.

Create Space—Through their services, you can sell books, CDs, and DVDs for a fraction of the cost of traditional manufacturing, while maintaining more control over your materials. They make it simple to distribute your books, music, and video through internet retail outlets, your own website, and other bookstores, retailers, libraries, and academic institutions.

Collaborative Book Publishing

Morgan James—Provides entrepreneurs with the vital information, inspiration, and guidance they need to be successful. Morgan James trademarked the term *entrepreneurial publisher* because of their unique collaborative approach with authors and other publishers, treating them as partners rather than solely as intellectual property suppliers or competitors.

Greenleaf—Designed to support the independent author. Makes it possible for writers to retain the rights to their work and still compete with the major publishing houses. They distribute their titles to major trade outlets, including bookstores, libraries, and airport retailers.

CD/DVD Creation

Disk.com—State-of-the-art manufacturing facilities providing full-service media replication/duplication, printing, packaging, warehousing, and media distribution. Customers range from individual customers to Fortune 500 corporations.

Kunaki—CD/DVD manufacturing, publishing, distributing, fulfilling, and shipping. No minimums or setup fees. Retail quality, full-color, glossy, fully assembled, cellophane-wrapped, high-quality, retail-ready products with free UPC bar codes. Drop-ship to any address. Just-in-time production. Automatic fulfillment. Accepts credit card orders on your behalf to instantly manufacture and ship your products to your customers.

Freelancers for Hire

Elance—A global, online staffing platform where companies, organizations, and individuals can hire independent freelance professionals and use online collaboration tools to manage teams and projects.

Fiverr—A global online marketplace offering tasks and services, referred to as "gigs" and micro-jobs, beginning at a cost of five dollars per job performed. Currently, Fiverr lists over one million services on the site that range between $5 and $500.

Conference Calls

Free Conferencing—Provides phone and web-based conferencing services with advanced tools including screen sharing and other collaboration tools. StartMeeting is a new audio and web conferencing service that incorporates features including screen sharing of files, spreadsheets, presentations, and other content. Includes cloud-based meeting recording and playback and a customizable online Meeting Wall.

Free Conference Call—Frees you from the hassles and expense of traditional call conferencing with simple, convenient, and reliable service at little or no cost.

Screencasting

ScreenFlow—Screencasting and video editing software for the Mac OS X operating system. It can capture the audio and video from the computer, edit the captured video, add highlights or annotation, and output a QuickTime video file.

Camtasia—More than a simple screen recorder, Camtasia helps you create professional videos easily. Use Camtasia to record on-screen activity, customize and edit content, add interactive elements, and share your videos with anyone on nearly any device. For PC or Mac.

Contest Plugins

Whishpond—A social contests plugin makes it easy to build and track contests on WordPress Sites, Facebook, Twitter, and mobile.

Votigo—Allows brands, agencies, and enterprises to acquire, engage, and manage their customers through a full social marketing suite that includes promotions, publisher, community management, applications, social CRM, and analytics.

Webinar

Easy Webinar Plugin—Turn your webinar into a webcast so you no longer need to be present. This shifts your webinar from active income to passive income. Create a webinar one time and have it play repeatedly based on the times you choose. Schedule your webinars to play in your time zone or your attendee's local time zone but still have the look and feel of a live webinar. Utilizes a software plugin with a onetime fee.

GoToWebinar—Conduct do-it-yourself webinars with up to one thousand people—all for one flat rate. Reduce travel while reaching larger audiences around the world.

Marketing Automation

Infusionsoft—All-in-one sales and marketing automation software for small businesses that combines CRM, email marketing, and e-commerce. Makes it easy for small businesses to get organized, attract more customers, grow sales, and save massive amounts of time.

OfficeAutopilot—All-in-one business and marketing platform designed for information marketers, experts, and coaches. By integrating your contact management, payment processing, automated marketing, task management, affiliate management, and much more, OfficeAutopilot makes an otherwise tangled mess of technology into a simple and powerful platform that's built for your growth.

Instant Customer—A revolutionary new way to communicate and follow up with your business connections, leads, customers, family, and friends. Create marketing campaigns that utilize all the traditional channels of lead generation such as phone, email, and web forms, and add in the game-changing new methods of mobile text marketing, business card scanning, direct-to-voicemail, autoresponders, teleseminars, and webinars.

Project Management

Basecamp—Keep track of every file, discussion, and event from beginning to end—all in one place. Web-based project management and collaboration tool. To-dos, files, messages, schedules, and milestones. (This is the framework Mike Rohde, the illustrator for this book, used to communicate with me to complete our project.)

Mindjet—Mindjet popularized Mindmapping, a virtual whiteboard. Track the status of tasks, post updates, and share and read comments in threaded conversations. Send out more detailed updates with easy-to-assemble progress reports. All of your tasks are prioritized and organized, and you're automatically notified of deadlines. Experience true collaboration with fewer meetings, calls, and emails, and complete your projects faster.

Physical Payments

Square—Accept credit card payments anywhere with your iPhone, Android, or iPad. Download the free Square app to get started.

Paypal Here—Accept credit cards, checks, and PayPal wherever your customers are on your iPhone, iPad, or Android devices.

Payment Gateway

Vanco—Specializes in electronic payment solutions. They provide secure and reliable processing for both recurring and onetime transactions.

Authorize.net—A payment gateway service provider that allows you to accept credit card and electronic check payments through their website and over an IP connection.

Online Shopping Cart

1ShoppingCart—Build a powerful, secure e-commerce storefront with their Online Store Software. Sell, promote, and grow with the Online Store Builder.

PayPal—A global e-commerce business allowing payments and money transfers to be made through the internet. Online money transfers serve as electronic alternatives to paying with traditional paper methods such as checks and money orders.

Email Services/Autoresponders

Mailchimp—Online email marketing solution to manage contacts, send emails, and track results. Offers plugins for other programs. It has 2.5 million users that collectively send over four billion emails a month through the service.

AWeber—Email marketing software that's easy to use and only a dollar to try. Send email newsletters and autoresponders. Top-notch email deliverability.

Constant Contact—Through its unique combination of online marketing tools and free personalized coaching, Constant Contact helps small businesses, associations, and nonprofits connect and engage with their next great customer, client, or member.

Website Themes

Thesis—Deploy (and tweak) your WordPress designs.

Optimize Press—Create marketing pages and membership sites in WordPress. An amazing and affordable onetime fee.

Membership Management Solutions

Wishlist Member—A powerful yet easy to use membership solution that can turn any WordPress blog into a full-blown membership site. Just unzip and upload the plugin, and within minutes you'll have your own membership site up and running, complete with protected, members-only content, integrated payments, and member management.

Digital Access Page—Create a fully automated "buyers only" site with onetime payments, recurring subscriptions, or no payments at all (free members). Built-in content responder (to drip content), email autoresponder and broadcast system, shopping cart with coupons, dime-sales, one-click upsells, and an affiliate program that instantly turns your members into a salesforce.

Kajabi—Quickly and painlessly post content online and charge for access to it. Easy-to-use platform that lets you quickly create beautiful membership sites, right in your web browser. Nothing to download or install. No hosting necessary.

Domain Registration and Hosting

BlueHost—Known as one of the largest web hosting companies, they also provide domain registration as well as many other products.

Video Production and Marketing

EasyVideoSuite—Build your lists fast. Attract an audience and increase your income from video.

LeadPlayer—Video player for online businesses and digital marketers.

Prepare for Your Product Launch

So, what did you think of the tool tour?

It can feel overwhelming at first. Because of this, I coach my clients to start small. Choose one product and go with it. Or start by watching a video tutorial and imagine the potential.

The creation process is interesting. At least for me, I become incredibly motivated once I've identified people who need my product. I create better and faster, knowing my product will help real people with real problems. Otherwise, like anybody, I tend to procrastinate and drag my heels.

Now is the perfect time to launch your products and increase your influence, impact, and income in the process. Get ready to find out why. In the next step (Step Six—Create Your Promotion), I'll share a few powerful principles that will unlock your creative potential.

Key Points

(If you RT, use #DJtoDJ to join the conversation with other DJs)

1. The more success you achieve, the less accessible you become.

2. DJs can keep adding more activity or they can increase their influence, impact, and income by creating products.

3. More activity yields active income and more product yields passive income.

4. Although creating product isn't necessary to join the DJs, passive income is.

5. If you want more freedom, finances, and fulfillment (the three benefits experienced by every DJ), then you need to create products.

6. Activity brings limits because of your own limitations—time, presence, and energy.

7. Products are limitless because they're not dependent upon your time, presence, or energy.

8. You can record your services now and later turn them into products that produce passive income.

9. The toughest part of creating your product is *the anticipation* of creating it.

10. Work expands to fill the time available for its completion.

11. The thing to be done swells in perceived importance and complexity in direct ratio with the time to be spent in its completion.

12. The more you think about a simple task, the more complex it becomes. Your anxiety and stress increase until the task is completed.

13. Start small. Choose one product and go with it.

14. Motivation comes once you've identified people who need your product.

15. You create better and faster when you know your product will help real people with real problems.

Step Six:
CREATE Your Promotion

Market before You Manufacture

> The only purpose of starting is to finish, and while the projects we do are never really finished, they must ship.
>
> Seth Godin

I liked Adam McCampbell. Anyone could see he was oozing with potential. Well-read, technologically savvy, highly networked, and a family man. He had everything going for him, except he was *stuck in his day job.*

This competent young professional worked as a sales rep for a reputable furniture brand. Although Adam achieved success in his position, he wasn't fulfilled.

Adam clearly had more in him. But at the moment he didn't have complete clarity.

No Product? No Problem!

By May 2012, I was ready. Although I knew for years I needed to leave my day job, I still lacked a few steps in my Dream Jobber Plan.

At that point, I had started to design my story, my service, and my space. I even created my platform. But clearly I didn't have a financially profitable product, much less a way to promote it.

I felt stuck.

But ever so slowly, I began to believe.

I no longer focused on all the *What ifs?* (What if I fail . . . ?)

Instead, I shifted my thinking to all of the *How can Is?* (How can I succeed . . . ?)

And because I believed, other people began to believe too.

I just finished writing my fifth book—*The Deeper Path*. I knew this book would give readers a huge shot of clarity toward successfully navigating their lives. But as traditionally published authors know, books release many months later. This was May 2012 and the book wouldn't come out until February 2013. What could I do with a book that wouldn't release for almost an entire year?

I dabbled with the idea of one day creating a coaching program around the book. I knew the content proved powerful, at least in my own life. And it solved a problem that paralyzed so many people—*lack of clarity.*

But in my private thoughts, I had an even bigger idea. Starting a Deeper Path Team.

My business partner David and I regularly heard transformational stories from the Your Secret Name team. We started that team a year and a half *after* the book released.

I thought about certifying people to coach and speak on *The Deeper Path* too. But this was nine months *before* the book came out. How could I promote it now?

Maybe I could market before I manufacture, I wondered.

But then I dismissed it promptly. *That's a stupid thought.*

Or was it?

Some Serious Sparks at Starbucks

I met Adam at Starbucks in Powell that morning. An undersized version compared to other Starbucks around, they still served green tea lattes and provided comfy chairs.

On the drive over, I made the intentional commitment to listen well. I felt Adam deserved my best and I wanted to *show up filled up*. I could have brought my own story into the conversation, but I wanted to serve him. I had several other mentors pouring into me at the time and I wanted to add value to Adam.

That morning I listened.

I asked questions.

I dug deeper.

And I what I heard impressed me.

Adam shared some of his dreams and goals. They felt real, raw, and unrefined. Although he lacked an action plan, I loved what I heard and I felt energized by his energy.

After about an hour, Adam commented on how helpful our chat had been. Putting words to his new world created enthusiasm and clarity. He asked if I knew any other young professionals who might want to gather for a mastermind. Maybe a group of like-minded people could help each other stay accountable to their dreams and goals.

That was all the motivation I needed.

I knew if Adam and I parted ways that day, his dreams might just sputter along for the next few years like mine did years before. He had identified his need and now he clearly wanted a solution. Little did he know I had just finished *The Deeper Path*, which was created specifically for people who needed clarity.

The last chapter of the book included a powerful coaching model (OPUS/CORE) developed by my friend and builder Chet Scott. This is the same Chet from chapter 1, who told me at Panera about his strange contentment.[1]

The funny thing is, the more clarity I discovered, the more contentment I felt in my own life. It wasn't so strange after all. This unconventional leader, who founded an unconventional company called Built to Lead, helped me clarify my own dream job and create a path to achieve it.

That morning I told Adam that I wanted to start a coaching group based on my new book. Although the book wouldn't release for another nine months, we could start the group anyway. With my mental juices flowing, I immediately thought of a few other young professionals I could invite.

We concluded our time with the understanding I'd recruit a few other folks and then pick a date. I told him the coaching group would involve a fee and it would last a certain amount of sessions. I didn't know much beyond those broad details.

I left the Starbucks and drove two minutes down the road to my financial advisor's office. I asked him if he had a few minutes to chat. Surprisingly he did.

I got right into it and asked him more about his dreams and goals. (He probably thought I seemed a little more amped then usual. I'll just blame it on the green tea latte though.) Although he knew his career goals, he admitted he needed more clarity with some personal goals. I invited him to join my new coaching cohort, which would start in four weeks. (In the two-minute drive over to his office I had picked the name "cohort" and a rough start date.)

He agreed and then offered his office as a meeting place for the cohort. I drove away from our stand-up meeting completely thrilled. When I got home, I then called a colleague named Will Zell, an incredibly successful businessman a couple towns over. I asked him about his dreams and goals. He shared them, but said he could use some help in the area of priorities. With six businesses and a young family, he wanted to prevent burnout.

I invited him to join The Deeper Path Coaching Cohort. (In the short drive home I had "branded" the new experience.) I also told him the location, the length of our cohort (ten sessions), and the price of the investment. He agreed.

I hung up the phone. Three for three! I felt completely ecstatic. I thought I'd better call my friend (now business partner) and let him know the good news.

"Hi David. It's Kary. Hope you're well. Um . . . we've got something we need to create. I have our first coaching group starting in four weeks. It's called The Deeper Path Coaching Cohort. We'd better get busy."

Your Product's Best Friend—The Promotion Path

Perhaps my story—marketing before you manufacture—sounds a bit unbelievable. But it's more common than you'd think.

Nearly every traditionally published book you read was marketed long before it was ever manufactured. Bookstores "buy" the book months before publication. They invest in the idea based on the integrity of the publisher, the reputation of the author, and the brief book description.

We could go back even further. The book idea is marketed by the agent to the publisher long before the book buyer ever hears about it. Traditional publishers even pay the author an advance *before* they see a completed manuscript. This is how creation works.

Consider other industries. Think about the last time you sat down to watch a movie at the theater. What appeared on the screen before the feature film?

Movie trailers—a whole bunch of them!

These trailers are a classic examples of marketing before manufacturing. Although the director filmed parts of the movie to produce the two-minute trailer, many other parts are undone, including the musical score and final edits. Still, they "sell" the movie long before it releases and astute audiences buy into it.

To help you market before you manufacture, I want to share what I call The Promotion Path. Apply these ten steps to your situation and you'll get moving faster.

I'll share these general principles within the context of The Deeper Path Coaching Cohort—one of my products—so it all makes sense. I figure seeing The Promotion Path in a real "case study" context will help drive the principles deeper.

The Promotion Path

1. **Connect the client.** People believe in people, not products.

2. **Market the message.** A great product tells a great story and solves a great problem.

3. **Identify the benefits.** How will this alleviate pain or add pleasure?

4. **Manufacture the product.** Real people really motivate you.

5. **Guarantee the experience.** Assume the risk and earn a sale.

6. **Trust the process.** Never, never, never give up.

7. **Overdeliver the value.** Exceed their expectations.

8. **Tweak the content.** Edits create credibility.

9. **Gather the testimonials.** It's your job to track the transformation.

10. **Envision the future.** Always communicate their next step.

1. Connect the Client

People believe in people, not products.

Maybe you've heard the phrase, "Telling isn't selling?"

Don't start by communicating your product. Instead, first connect with your potential customer. Take time to understand them and their relevant needs. If your product connects with their needs, only then connect them to your product. If not, don't.

When we promoted the Cohorts I took time to understand the needs of my potential clients. If I believed my product didn't address their needs, then I didn't offer it. Instead, I found them another solution even if it wasn't my own product. DJs earn the reputation of being helpful. Because I earned their trust first (with no strings attached), many times I earned their sale months later.

2. Market the Message

A great product tells a great story and solves a great problem.

Don't underestimate the value of your product. A paper clip or nail clipper solves a great problem when you truly need one. If you think little of your product, others will too. Albert Einstein warned, "If you put a small value on yourself, rest assured that the world will not raise your price."[2]

DJs integrate their GPS into their product. When we created the Cohort, I wove my Guru Positioning Story (GPS) right into it. My product immediately became achievable, believable, and conceivable. I conveyed tremendous belief the Cohort would solve their need for clarity. If people pushed back, I pushed back harder. Of course, I couched my push-back with kindness and grace. However, I didn't back down. I didn't let clichés or platitudes create space between them and their potential.

3. Identify the Benefits

How will this alleviate pain or add pleasure?

Products require an investment. If you expect customers to part with their money and/or time, then you'd better make the investment worthwhile.

We clearly identified how the Cohorts would alleviate pain and add pleasure. We published this content in a variety of formats. Initially we created a "one sheet"—a single document that summarizes a product for publicity and sales. Then we placed this content on our website and later into a squeeze page video.[3] You can see many more examples at DayJobtoDreamJob.com.

4. Manufacture the Product

Real people really motivate you.

Many DJs share a similar experience. When they "sell" their first product, immediately something inside their brain switches. They go from extreme doubter to firm believer. Sometimes, a real person is all the motivation you need to create the product.

After the first sale, if you still don't have the product created do what many DJs do. Depending on the industry, they "buy" the necessary time to create the product by offering more value. They ask for a couple weeks before delivery or promise additional bonuses, extra features, upgraded elements, and so forth. You know your offer and your industry. Just be sure to maintain your integrity throughout the process. And always give more value than expected.

David and I used Mondays to create the lesson for each Friday. We enjoyed the pressure because we knew our audience depended on us. (Talk about motivated guys on a mission.) Our first Cohort manual was completely digital. Attendees would download the upcoming lesson or print out a hard copy. We never missed a deadline and we put our whole selves into the product.

5. Guarantee the Experience

Assume the risk and earn a sale.

Great products back up their claim with a guarantee. As you learned from Step Three—Design Your Service, you can choose three types of guarantees: the standard guarantee, the extended time period guarantee, or the risk reversal guarantee. Studies show by including a guarantee you increase the number of sales. Customers enjoy the confidence and security a promise brings.

We included a thirty-day guarantee with our Cohort. We allowed attendees to experience nearly half of the content (four out of ten sessions) before making up their minds. If they were unhappy, we refunded their money, plus an extra $100. We also absorbed any credit card fees.

To this date we only had two guys ask for their money back. One quit before we started. The other, an international attendee, dropped out when the language barrier proved too difficult to understand the content. We returned their money promptly and gladly.

6. Trust the Process

Never, never, never give up.

Along the way obstacles will appear. Anticipate glitches, hang-ups, and setbacks. But be assured, it gets easier. Maintain a positive attitude and keep pumping out productive action. Don't get sidelined by self-limiting beliefs or mental drama. Remember the *why* and you will find a way.

David and I committed to keep moving forward. Our first Cohort turned into our second, then our third, then our twenty-fourth. We eventually added online Cohorts (digital) to our onsite Cohorts (physical). Today hundreds of people from all different countries and continents participate in our Cohorts. This expansion brought additional adjustments, but we welcome the growth. Our Cohort alumni have evolved into a passionate tribe that still keeps encouraging one another to this day.

7. Overdeliver the Value

Exceed their expectations.

Underperforming on expectations creates disappointment. Overdelivering creates delight. Knowing our Cohorts function as an early step in our sales funnel, we're completely committed to overwhelming our customers with more value than they imagine.

Today's Cohorts are much more robust than our first one, with Adam. Although our early Cohorts contained six people, we've had some consist of twenty attendees. We quickly realized coaching everyone on these live calls was impossible. As a result, David filmed ten hours of me teaching *The Deeper Path* content. He then created an online university with a digital framework (we use Kajabi as our digital framework).

A video "drops" each week and attendees can comment on the content or their specific situation. Attendees love the combination of recorded teaching and live coaching calls. In addition we include special bonuses, a private Facebook group, and a forty-page coaching manual. Our alumni often tell us we don't charge enough for the value we provide.

8. Tweak the Content

Edits create credibility.

Nobody gets it perfect the first time and so you have a choice. You can either wait until it's perfect (and it never will be) or you can publish it and tweak it along the way. Every DJ struggles sending his or her imperfect "baby" out into the world. But DJs do and that's what separates them from Day Jobbers.

Seth Godin explains more:

> Perfect doesn't mean flawless. Perfect means it does exactly what I need it to do. A vacation can be perfect even if the nuts on the plane weren't warmed before serving. Any project that's held up in revisions and meetings and general fear-based polishing is the victim of a crime. It's a crime because you're stealing that perfect work from a customer who will benefit from it. You're holding back the good stuff from the people who need it, afraid of what the people who don't will say. Stop polishing and ship instead. Polished perfect isn't better than perfect, it's merely shinier. And late.[4]

David and I made the conscious decision to "ship." We knew our customers needed our content and we were going to deliver it. Of course flaws and errors emerged along the way. Think of it as an extended beta release. (Don't forget, Google's "beta" lasted more than five years.[5])

View your customer as a traveler wandering in the desert, in desperate need of your water. Could you take longer polishing the glass before serving them the water? Sure. Do they care? Not that much.

9. Gather the Testimonials

It's your job to track the transformation.

You must start somewhere, and usually before you receive your first testimonial. Stop making excuses. Someone you know will vouch for your content. Collect as you go. Ask for it. Give them a deadline. Write it for them. Let them tweak it and make it their own. Put their picture with their endorsement. When you overdeliver the value, your customers will trip over themselves trying to give you testimonials. Do your job first. They'll do theirs next.

David and I committed to deliver the best value possible. When we asked for testimonials they came flooding in. Here's an easy method. Create your product on LinkedIn, find your client, and then click "Request Recommendation." They'll be sent a request that takes them sixty seconds to complete. Prepare them beforehand by verbally asking permission first.

Here's an example of our page on LinkedIn (http://bit.ly/dpcohort) and a sample testimonial below:

Barry L. Smith—Owner at Building What Matters, Portland, Oregon, Area

Do you truly know what your purpose is and are you living it out? The experience of going through a Deeper Path Cohort changed my life. Understanding my purpose with absolute clarity has brought me to a new level of awareness that I never thought possible. The collaboration with my Cohort was invaluable and I am now connected to like-minded people who both encouraged and empowered me through the process. Join a Cohort now and author your own OPUS!

10. Envision the Future

Always communicate their next step.

DJs realize their products are a long-term relationship. Businesses that skimp on value only experience the initial sale. Then they spend the rest of their time and money filling the top of the funnel over and over.

Businesses that value their customers earn trust over time. They experience repeat customers and lifelong fans. Many get hounded by their customers who anxiously await their next product release. They anticipate the next product that will alleviate their pain or increase their pleasure. Don't believe me? Just ask Apple and their raving fans waiting for their next release.

We knew if we exceeded expectations, a portion of our alumni would want to be certified on the content. We were right. David and I created The Deeper Path Team, which rewarded our coaches. They keep 100 percent of their profits. Before the book even launched in February 2013, we had more than 160 Cohort alumni, more than fifty *Deeper Path* coaches, and more than $100,000 in sales.

We told our alumni their next step was to join The Deeper Path Team or The Deeper Path Fellowship. Even more valuable than the coaches and the dollars, we received dozens of stories that detailed specific examples of life change. Check out our Team page and see for yourself (DeeperPathBook.com/team).

Don't Wait for Product before You Promote!

Guess I'm glad we didn't sit around nine months waiting before we promoted our product. Our delay would have sabotaged our influence, impact, and income.

Expect to feel fear. But this is why it's the right thing to do. Fear reminds you you're alive. It's time to market before you manufacture and promote before you produce.

I think I owe Adam a green tea latte.

I guess our little chat catapulted both of us closer to our dream jobs. Time to have your own little chat with yourself.

Key Points

(If you RT, use #DJtoDJ to join the conversation with other DJs)

1. To paraphrase Seth Godin, the only purpose of starting is to finish, and while the projects we do are never really finished, they must ship.

2. Change your *What ifs* to *How can Is*.

3. When you meet with potential clients, show up filled up. Make it about them, not you.

4. Connect with your potential customer before you communicate your product.

5. Don't allow clichés or platitudes to create space between your customers and their potential.

6. If you expect customers to part with their money and/or time, then you'd better make the investment worthwhile.

7. When you "sell" your first product, immediately something inside your brain switches. You go from extreme doubter to firm believer.

8. Studies show including a guarantee increases the number of sales.

9. Don't get sidelined by self-limiting beliefs or mental drama. Remember the *why* and you will find a way.

10. Underperforming expectations creates disappointment. Overdelivering creates delight.

11. You can either wait until its perfect (and it *never* will be) or you can ship it and tweak it along the way.

12. Every DJ struggles with sending their imperfect "baby" out into the world.

13. Flaws and errors will emerge along the way. Think of it as an extended beta release. Don't forget, Google's "beta" lasted more than five years.

14. When you overdeliver the value, your customers will trip over themselves trying to give you testimonials.

15. Businesses that skimp on value only experience the initial sale. DJs realize their products are a long-term relationship.

Step Seven:
MAINTAIN Your Community

Every Dream Needs a Team

If you want to build a ship, don't drum up people together to collect wood and don't assign them tasks and work, but rather teach them to long for the endless immensity of the sea.

Antoine de Saint-Exupery

Brandon Clements loved writing.[1] He wrote all through college. And even after he jumped into a "real" job, the writing bug still infected him. Brandon wanted to write a book, and so he did.

When he mentioned his idea to an editor from a major publisher, they kindly declined his manuscript. According to the editor, his platform wasn't big enough. Besides that, his content didn't help him.

Brandon wrote a fictional story that felt too "religious" for secular publishers. Ironically, it also felt too "secular" for religious publishers. His manuscript, *Every Bush Is Burning*, seemed like it was in its own category.

Aware of the obvious, Brandon took action. He self-published and officially claimed his own category.

Communities Will Kickstart

After researching printers, Brandon landed on Lightning Source. He added a Kickstarter campaign that provided tools to raise funds for the project.

Kickstarter makes crowd funding easy. In their own words, they're

A home for everything from films, games, and music to art, design, and technology. Kickstarter is full of projects, big and small, that are brought to life. Since our launch in 2009, 5.4 million people have pledged $920 million, funding more than 53,000 creative projects. Thousands of creative projects are raising funds on Kickstarter right now.[2]

Besides generous friends who supported his Kickstarter campaign, Brandon also had a number of talented friends who helped him create a crisp website and an engaging trailer.[3]

And in October 2011, his friends rallied around him and together they launched *Every Bush Is Burning* in his own city. However, although people gobbled up a couple hundred copies initially, after nine months Brandon had only sold five hundred copies.

More than the money, Brandon cared about the message. Nobody wants their brainchild to sit untouched. Although the book injected hope into his readers, not enough people knew about it.

Feeling despair, Brandon knew he needed a spark.

He met Jeff Goins, a popular author and blogger at a conference.[4] They immediately became friends. Jeff couldn't see any difference between Brandon's book and a traditionally published book. He thought it looked *that* amazing.

Regardless, Brandon's book lacked momentum. Confiding in Jeff, Brandon explained his dilemma. Jeff suggested he try a program called KDP Select.[5] Essentially, enrolling in this program would make *Every Bush Is Burning* free for a limited time. Readers worldwide would be permitted to download a free digital version.

Jeff had heard of an author who used the program and gave away six hundred copies of her book in just one weekend. Brandon knew his book needed some fire, and so he decided to give it a shot. Just before enrolling in the program, he guest posted on Jeff's blog and on AuthorMarketingClub.com to inform people about the free download.

Then he waited.

At lunchtime on the first day of the free download, Brandon looked at his statistics. He couldn't believe it. His book had been downloaded *five thousand* times in just a few hours. As the days rolled by he held the #2 spot on the Kindle store. And by the end of the fifth day, his book was downloaded over sixty thousand times!

He was blown away by the response, and stories of impact swept into his inbox. People immediately posted over one hundred reader reviews. The week following the free KDP select campaign, he sold over two thousand additional copies.

Although his results might be uncharacteristic, Brandon didn't complain.

One reader in his own hometown discovered the book, and since reading it has joined the small group Brandon and his wife lead. She's now experiencing the message of the book firsthand, finding healing from her painful past.

Besides replying to comments from his new fans, Brandon also found himself replying to responses from publishers. Evidently, they're now interested in his future writing career. Seems like his growing community surprised them just as much as it did him.

Time for Team Building

If you're going to escape your day job, you're going to need some help. DJs know every dream needs a team. But in this endeavor, you must also be selective.

In *The Shawshank Redemption*, Andy found a true friend in Red. By his own admission, Red said, "There's a con like me in every prison in America, I guess. I'm the guy who can get it for you."[6]

That's exactly what Red did. He got Andy a number of things he needed to escape, including a rock hammer. Yet besides Red, Andy benefited from a number of other teammates, including:

Heywood—he gave Andy rope.

Brooks—he gave Andy a poster.

Captain Hadley—he gave Andy protection.

Andy's escape was clearly a team effort. Yours will be too.

Cherish your team. Value them. Buy them lunch. Send them cards. Donate blood to them. Be generous. Maintaining your community is not only intelligent, it's also essential. Every DJ needs four types of strategic teammates.

Four Types of Teammates

1. **Fans**—the people who believe in you.
2. **Freelancers**—the people who work with you.
3. **Friends**—the people who vouch for you.
4. **Funders**—the people who invest in you.

1. Fans

Fans are followers. Although their motivation may be different, on some level they all believe in you. There are three different types of fans.

Consumers—the takers. These fans hang around because they're hungry. Maybe your content feeds them for noble reasons. Maybe they steal it for their own gain. Regardless of their intent, don't let them bother you. Celebrate the fact they follow you. Seth Godin gives us great perspective—piracy isn't our enemy, obscurity is.[7]

Contributors—the sharers. These fans RT you on Twitter and share your posts on Facebook. They follow you and spread your message. Their comments fuel you and their critiques push you.

Collaborators—the givers. These fans are rare. Some call them superfans. They can't wait for your next product, post, or podcast. When you ask for help, they're always first in line.

2. Freelancers

You can't do it all, nor should you. Find quality people to hire. If you're on a tight budget, consider exchanging your services for theirs. Freelancers fill two categories.

Generalists—they do what you could do. In Dream Job Bootcamp, I coach clients to determine their per-hour value. This is tough for some to do, but that's another topic. Once they settle on an hourly value, we do an inventory of their schedules, both personally and professionally. We look for areas where they can save time and money. I'll give you an example.

Let's imagine Susie determines her value at $50 an hour. While exploring her week, we discover she wants to order firewood for the winter. The firewood company will deliver the wood for free, but they charge $25 an hour to stack the wood. The company estimates her firewood will take them one hour to stack. Should Susie pay for the wood to be stacked, or should she stack it herself? Although she has freelance work to do, she wants to save the $25 so she decides to stack the wood herself.

By the time she fills up the air in her wheelbarrow tire, locates her gloves, and laces her boots, she's already got one hour invested. Because she's not used to the labor, it ends up taking her three hours to stack the wood instead of one.

This job, which could have cost her $25, ended up costing her much more—$175 more to be exact. Here's the breakdown:

Value per Hour	Time to Complete Job	Total Cost for Job
Firewood Company = $25	1 Hour	$25
Susie's Freelance = $50	4 Hours	$200

(When I've shared this example with audiences, women have told me I failed to factor cleanup time. Turns out hair and makeup can add more time to the illustration. I stand corrected and enlightened.)

By knowing your value, you can outsource unprofitable tasks by delegating them to others. When you focus on the best return for your work, you can increase your influence, impact, and income at a much faster rate. If you choose, you can invest your extra time with the people and tasks most important to you.

Consider hiring a virtual assistant to do the tasks you can do but choose not to do. (Two sites worth checking out: eahelp.com and elance.com.) Assistants (virtual or physical) can do the following work: secretarial tasks, regular transcription, medical transcription, customer service, data entry, graphics, writing, administrative support, editing, proofreading, blogging, chat support, research, tech support, website help, technical or other legitimate work at home.

Your tribe is depending upon you to do what only you can do. Outsource everything else.

Specialists—**they do what you can't do.** Why spend dozens of hours learning to do what someone else can do in a matter of minutes? Look on Fiverr or Elance. People rank freelancers based on their performance in previous projects. Read the reviews and eliminate the risk. Filter the talent based on the recommendations.

3. Friends

These are not Facebook "friends." I'm referring to a different type—three different types, to be exact.

Truth Tellers—**they call you out.** These friends earn the right to speak into your life. They care enough to say it straight. Although tough to hear, their insight makes you better.

Edifiers—**they draw you in.** These friends throw sunshine your way. Their good vibes draw you in and their positivity frees you from any funk you might feel. Be prepared to get unstuck.

Challengers—**they push you up.** These friends see your potential even better than you do. They love you unconditionally and challenge you to rise up to the epic opportunity before you.

A balanced team contains all three types of friends.

4. Funders

A dream team needs specific resources. But don't only think of money. You need three types of investors.

Time Investors. My best funders are people who've invested their time in me. People like Angela Scheff, who taught me about publishing. Or Chris Fabry and Tim Willard, who taught me about ghostwriting. These strategic conversations yielded tremendous dividends. To this day, I'm humbled by their generous hearts.

Who do you need to spend time with? Why do you need their time? If they agree to chat, come prepared. Do your research. Print out your questions. Take notes. Send a follow-up thank-you. Tell them how you applied their advice. Respect these funders by honoring their time.

Treasure Investors. Although money is often perceived as the biggest obstacle, it's truly the least of your worries. We'll explore how to make money in Step Nine—Maintain Your Credibility. For the time being, understand you can ask others to invest in you financially. Many people use Kickstarter as a venue. However, I'm not a big fan of asking for treasure investors. This can complicate your day job escape. Although over the years I've received a financial gift on a rare occasion, I don't solicit funds. It's not my style nor my business model. You may disagree.

Talent Investors. These funders give their brains, not their wallets. Consider creating a Personal Advisory Board. I've had one the last ten years. I handpicked leaders who excel in areas I don't. Currently, I have a lawyer, a CPA, and a former bank analyst on my board. I've had pastors and business owners in the past. These board members have rotated on and off throughout the years.

The Personal Advisory Board Simple Structure

Here's one way to form your board. Use the Personal Advisory Board Simple Structure by filling in the blanks.

WHO—I'm going to ask _____ to serve on my board because
_____.

WHAT—This board will achieve the following goals: _____
_____. (Create a few initial agenda items, such as form an LLC, give prayer or encouragement, write a grant, publish a book.)

WHEN—This board will meet _____ (times per year. I suggest quarterly) for this amount of time _____ . (start time/end time. I suggest one-hour meetings.)

WHERE—We will meet at _____. (Meeting at a restaurant or with food involved causes too many distractions.)

WHY—We will meet for the clear purpose of: _____. (This shouldn't change.)

HOW—We will review old business and tackle the new agenda each meeting. (Have someone take notes. Always email the new agenda before the meeting.)

Through a one-on-one conversation, invite each leader to join your advisory board. Use the Personal Advisory Board Simple Structure as talking points. Ask them to invest four hours over the next year in making your dream a reality (one hour-long meeting, once per quarter). Tell them specifically why you want them to serve in this role. Ask them to think on it. Give them a deadline. And be sure to run your meetings *exactly opposite* of the Epically Bad Meetings we talked about earlier. (That way they'll stay.)

Time Out and Huddle Up

Enough talk. It's time to maintain your community. Start taking inventory of all the amazing people in your awareness. Invite them to step up and step out. Your dream needs a team.

Key Points

(If you RT, use #DJtoDJ to join the conversation with other DJs)

1. The best teams are selective and strategic.
2. Maintaining your team is essential. Shower them with gratitude.
3. Seth Godin puts it well—piracy isn't your enemy, obscurity is.

4. If you're on a tight budget, consider exchanging your services with other freelancers.

5. Know your hourly value.

6. Take an inventory of your schedule, both personally and professionally. Look for areas where you can save time and money.

7. Focus on the best return for your work, and increase your influence, impact, and income at a much faster rate.

8. Consider hiring a virtual assistant to do the tasks you can do but choose not to do.

9. Your tribe is depending upon you to do what only you can do. Outsource everything else.

10. Truth tellers are tough to hear, but their insight makes you better.

11. Challengers love you unconditionally and challenge you to rise up to the epic opportunity before you.

12. Respect time investors by honoring their time.

13. Form your board by using the Personal Advisory Board Simple Structure.

14. Run your meetings *exactly opposite* of the Epically Bad Meetings explained in earlier.

15. Personally invite people to join your dream team. Tell them why you want them to serve in this role.

Step Eight:
MAINTAIN Your Clarity

Complexity Kills Clarity

> One does not accumulate but eliminate. It is not daily increase but daily decrease. The height of cultivation always runs to simplicity.
>
> Bruce Lee

Adam McCampbell bravely said no.

His newfound clarity made the choice simple. Just six months ago, caught up in complexity, he might have jumped at the impressive promotional perks offered by his generous employer:

A company car

A six-figure salary

Incredible benefits

A robust expense account

A flexible schedule

But by authoring his OPUS in The Deeper Path Coaching Cohort, he achieved incredible clarity. Now he knew exactly what he wanted. And it didn't include spending half his week away from his young family.

Through a compelling process, Adam discovered his true purpose—*fueling leaders' dreams by creating high-performing teams.* Taking on the new role of managing furniture sales reps at his day job didn't fulfill that purpose. No matter how much they offered to pay him, he was out.

Although his dreams had felt unrefined only months before, today they were incredibly clear.

Four weeks before this offer of a promotion, he stood before our Cohort and read us part of his OPUS.[1] We couldn't believe his clarity. My guess is you won't either.

Adam McCampbell
OPUS—My Big Dream

The alarm buzzes at 6:00 a.m. I stretch, rub my face with water, and start a cup of coffee. Before my 7:00 a.m. workout I spend a quiet moment praying and meditating on God's ancient Scripture. After my workout I feel hungry and tired, but good.

At 9:30 a.m. I have a conference call with a CEO of a midsized manufacturing company. I've known him well for two years; we really got to know each other spending time with our boys at the Masters in the spring. We talk lightly and then I push him a bit on an accountability issue he's having with his CIO. After some heated discussion, he concedes my point and commits to call him out at their next one-to-one on Friday. They both will grow. We placed the CIO six months ago; he's good, but a bit headstrong.

Mike reminds me that the company is doing a company community day next weekend, cleaning up the local park, and wants the family to come with me. "We'll be there," I say before hanging up the phone. Mike's company has grown by 22 percent over the last sixteen months and the culture is so different, people love coming to work and really get into community days.

I meet [my wife] Chanelle at a favorite little restaurant downtown for lunch. We have a planning date. We are taking the entire family to Italy in two months and have some details to work out. She is so excited. She knows it will be a challenge, but after our European trip three years ago she wanted the whole family to experience a similar trip before they hit college.

In the afternoon I sneak away to a coffee shop to put the final touches on a talk I'm giving in Atlanta in October at the Catalyst Conference. It's not a lot of work since it's based on my most recent book, *Talent Farming*.

I can't wait to catch up with [my business partner] Alec next week, once he gets back from the World Cup with Cameron. It had to be a great trip seeing the United States win! We need to go over the launch of our fourth office in Denver. There is still a lot to do, but it will come together. I get an email on my phone from another great client. They average two hundred résumés a week and do not have any posted openings. It's due to the most recent spot in *INC* magazine highlighting their amazing hiring, onboarding, training, and people plan, which I'm proud to say we developed with them. The portion that got the most attention was the company-sponsored sabbatical employees could take to help find their "voice."

Later that afternoon [my son] Hudson and I work on our short game on our green in the backyard. He tells me who he's taking to prom, a great girl from our church. I delight in the excitement in his voice. At dinner we discuss our days in detail and [my son] Harrison talks feverishly about working on our most recent real estate project after school. I partnered with the boys to help put some money toward college and teach them a bit. My brothers are going to help us paint this weekend. I hate painting but I love the fellowship.

That night, Chanelle and I turn the television off early and spend some time talking more about our trip and reading travel websites. As I head to bed I whisper thanks to the Father for all he has done and is doing in my life.

Clarity Comes with a Cost

There's a danger in clarity.

Adam discovered this firsthand. Once you know what you want, you're dissatisfied with anything less. Why get paid to do something you don't want to do? Sounds like "professional prostitution" to me.

Rereading Adam's dream, you won't find anything about a furniture brand. And you won't see anything about abandoning his two boys for 50 percent of their childhood. Quite the opposite, you see an author, a business partner, and a man connected to his faith. You see a man deeply tied to his wife and sons.

Because of this clarity, Adam escaped his day job, despite their

generous offer. Instead, he entered his dream job full-time with VisionSpark cofounder Alec Broadfoot. With VisionSpark, a consulting
firm that specializes in finding companies superstar employees, Adam
turned his part-time passion into his full-time gig.

With Alec and Adam steering the ship, VisionSpark changes the
way many companies now hire. By incorporating the Choosing Win-
ners System, VisionSpark consistently puts up impressive numbers:

95 percent success rate

Average employee tenure is over seven years

150 to 300 percent increase in productivity

Increased employee morale

95 percent repeat business rate

99 percent satisfaction rate

Guaranteed results[2]

Alec found a competent cofounder in Adam. But the transition
came with a cost. Adam had to "decide" to walk away. He couldn't
hang on to his day job and simultaneously jump into his dream job.

Decide is an interesting word. We use it casually, but it carries some
serious weight. Decide comes from the Latin word *decidere*, which
means "to cut off." Its relative, *caedere*, means "to cut" or "to kill."

So when you make a decision, you're literally "killing your options."
You're cutting off other opportunities and possibilities.

This is why decisions are often so difficult. You know decisions
come with a cost and so you delay making them. You think delaying
solves the problem, but it only prolongs the pain.

What you fail to realize is that *not* making a decision is actually
a decision. You'll never have the exact same opportunity again. And
by choosing not to decide, you choose to stay exactly where you are.

When we finally do make a decision, we feel a loss. This small
death must be grieved appropriately. When Adam *decided* not to accept the generous offer, he *killed* his chances of moving up through
the ranks at his day job.

But this necessary death created the necessary space to enter his
new endeavor. Killing his day job gave birth to his dream job.

Similar to the flying trapeze artist who feels the rush of the temporary free fall, letting go of your day job and jumping for your dream job requires a certain confidence. Don't think blind faith. Imagine intentional clarity.

We call this The Deeper Path Payoff.

The Deeper Path Payoff

Walk the complete path and you'll experience success and significance. Take a shortcut and find yourself skimping or scamming.

Let's explore this path.

Clarity. Like Adam, all DJs experience deeper levels of clarity. This isn't where you begin, but it's definitely where you end up. Clarity comes before you take a step. Feeling restless in your day job isn't the signal to jump into your dream job. Not yet. No one will buy from you until you know your value and your products/services.

Competence. Something magical happens when you gain clarity. You become more aware of your strengths and weaknesses. You understand your few gifts with razor-sharp intuition. When you don't know your unique skills, it's a clear indication you're still unclear. And when you're unclear, no one will buy from you. Why would they? For example, try pulling up to a drive-thru restaurant. Ask what they're serving and how much it costs. If they're unclear, you'll drive away. And so will your potential customers.

Confidence. True confidence is simply the byproduct of clarity and competence. When you know your products/services, your value, and your ability to deliver results, you naturally communicate belief. People buy belief. Hardly something you conjure up, confidence flows from proven character. Notice how arrogance and confidence are diametrically opposed.

Arrogance	Confidence
Shows off = devious	Shows up = dependable
Deficit: created by negative self-image	Surplus: created by positive self-image
"Look at me."	"Let me look at you."
"How can you serve my wants?"	"How can I serve your needs?"

Influence. By embodying clarity, competence, and confidence, you earn the right to be heard. People invest in you by *paying* attention. Remember, time is even more valuable than money. When people allow you to influence them, it's because they see your unique value. Don't stop here. Keep walking the path.

Impact. When you reach this point, provide people a true solution for their problems. Give away your best for free. Assume the risk. Alleviate their pain or increase their pleasure. Connect with them before communicating your product/service. Let them taste the results for themselves. Watch what happens.

Income. If you travel this path slowly and sincerely, you'll discover it's the fastest way to true income. Get-rich schemes leave a bitter aftertaste. The Deeper Path Payoff puts you in the guru position surrounded by a tribe that really cares for you. Serve others. Provide true value. Offer real solutions for people's problems and they'll fight to invest in you.

Complexity Kills Clarity

One last thing before we take the final step. Many DJs crash and burn due to complexity. Stay simple. Listen to your Personal Advisory Board. But follow your intuition. You must live with your choices. Own up to them.

Many voices will give their opinions. They'll tell you what you need based on their experience, conventional wisdom, and stereotypical sound bites. But ask yourself, *Do I want their results?*

Conventional wisdom is conventional for a reason. DJs chart their own course. Don't be stupid or reckless, but don't invite complexity.

I purposefully avoid hiring employees, occupying an office, or investing in costly overhead. For me it works. I filter all my business decisions through my OPUS, a simple document I've posted for anyone to read (DeeperPathBook.com/team/).

My OPUS helps me "decide" what to say yes to and what to say no to. Chet Scott, the creator of OPUS, describes it as:

O Overarching Vision

P Purpose

U Unifying Strategies

S Scorecard for Significance[3]

I Keep It Simple

I do insane workouts, but only a few times a week. I eat healthy and worship daily. I love playing with my three kids.

My wife, Kelly, is a gift from above. She supports me and kicks my butt. She's my truth teller, edifier, and challenger all in one.

I do selective corporate gigs and I started a nonprofit. I write, coach, and speak. I love synergistic partnerships.

I have a few close friends and I love my tribe. My passion is Igniting Souls.

Like I said, simple.

Maintain clarity. Kill complexity.

Key Points

(If you RT, use #DJtoDJ to join the conversation with other DJs)

1. There's a danger in clarity. Once you know what you want, you're dissatisfied with anything less.

2. Getting paid to do something you don't want to do is professional prostitution.

3. You can't hang on to your day job and simultaneously jump into your dream job.

4. When you make a decision, you literally "kill your options" by cutting off other opportunities.

5. Delaying decisions doesn't solve the problem, it only prolongs the pain.

6. By choosing not to make a decision, you choose to stay exactly where you are.

7. Feeling restless in your day job isn't the signal it's time to jump into your dream job.

8. You must know your value and your products/services.

9. When you don't know your unique skills it's a clear indication you're still unclear. And when you're unclear, no one will buy from you.

10. True confidence is simply the byproduct of clarity and competence.

11. Confidence flows from proven character.

12. By embodying clarity, competence, and confidence, you earn the right to be heard.

13. Provide people with a true solution for their problems. Give away your best for free. Assume the risk. Alleviate their pain or increase their pleasure.

14. Serve others. Provide true value. Offer real solutions for people's problems and they'll fight to invest in you.

15. Complexity kills clarity.

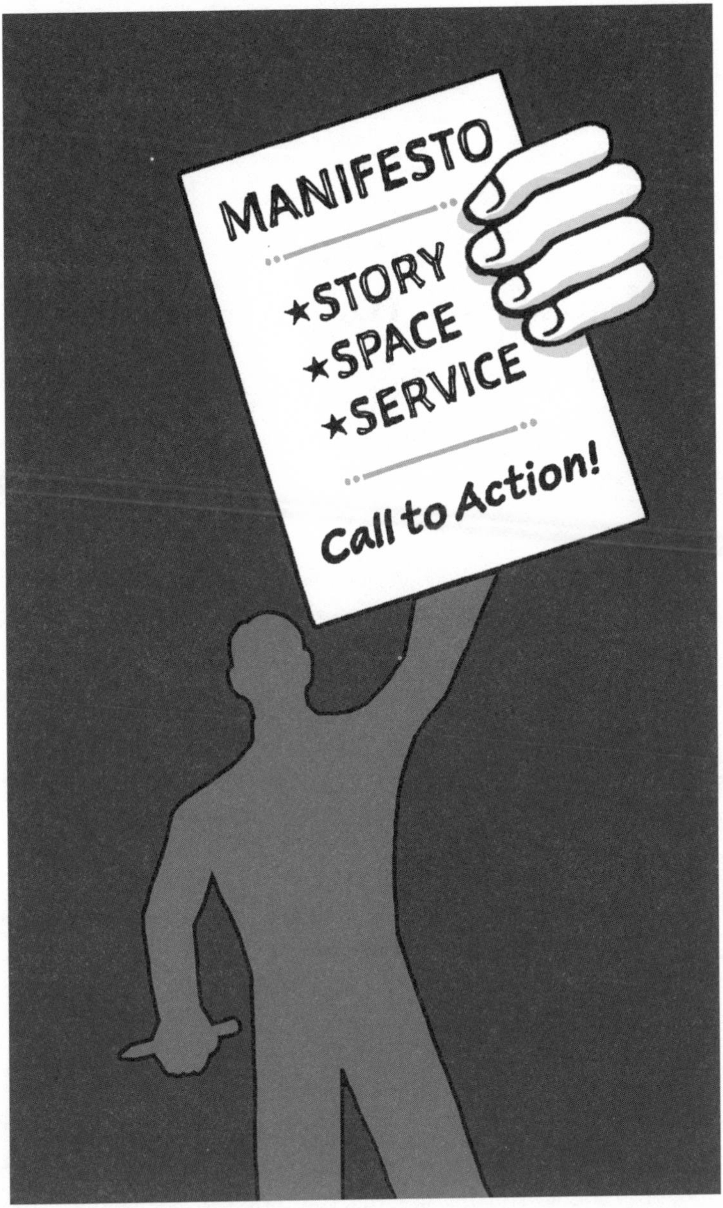
MANIFESTO
★STORY
★SPACE
★SERVICE
Call to Action!

Step Nine:
MAINTAIN Your Credibility

Success Is Found in Singularity

It's so easy to string together a bunch of platitudes. . . .
But what happens if you actually have a specific mission,
a culture in mind, a manifesto for your actions?

Seth Godin

Success is interesting. The more you chase it, the faster it flees from you. Success isn't something you achieve. It's someone you become.

But cutting to the chase, how do we become successful?

Here's what I know—true success begins and ends with credibility. I'll demonstrate with a quick illustration. Think of a certain radio station in your area. What do they play?

Pop?

Oldies?

Rock?

Suppose one day you tune into that station and hear something completely unexpected. For example, let's imagine you like country music.

(You might really have to use your *imagination*.) But let's also imagine you turn to that country music station and you hear rap instead.

Perplexed, you wait a couple of days.

Next time you turn to the same "country" station you hear classical music instead. After a short time, you'd lose both interest and respect.

Here's why. Conflicting "frequencies" create confusion. Worse than that, they also erode credibility.

Often unintentionally, we see this played out daily, especially through social media.

Give it a try. Subscribe to someone's Facebook status updates and listen for their frequency:

7 a.m.—Ranting about government and global warming.

10 a.m.—Posting his high score from the latest Facebook game.

12 p.m.—Linking to an article about new homeschool initiatives.

5 p.m.—Uploading a monster truck picture from the auto show downtown.

7 p.m.—Cursing the "bad" service experienced at a local restaurant.

10 p.m.—Announcing a new product line within his alarm system business.

If this guy's updates were a radio station or television program, he'd be out on the street before noon on his first day.

Remember, you are your business. People don't buy *from* you. They buy *you*. When you use social media to communicate mixed frequencies you confuse people. And when you confuse them you lose them.

People only follow brands they trust. Nobody pops open a Coca-Cola expecting to pour out 7-Up. Do that a few times, and you can kiss success—and stock value—good-bye.

Singularity attracts. Confusion repels.

What Song Are You Singing?

When I first began my business I was like that confusing country radio station. I didn't know what frequency I broadcasted. To say it kindly, I was still finding myself. But to say it bluntly, I was repelling potential customers.

By the term *frequency* I mean intentional and unintentional attitudes, behaviors, and messages you broadcast to the world around you. And I'm not exaggerating in the least. Scientific studies prove that every living being broadcasts a vibrational frequency.

Women know this well. Oftentimes they'll comment to their friends about a creepy guy giving them bad *vibes*. But vibes come in multiple forms, good and bad. In 1966 the American band the Beach Boys acknowledged the existence of positive vibes in their song "Good Vibrations."

Vibrations attract or repel on a conscious and subconscious level. The more credibility, the more attraction. The less credibility, the less attraction.

When I began, despite my best intentions and a strong emphasis on integrity, I still lacked credibility. You could say I lacked *brand* integrity. Credibility flows from singularity, and I didn't have much of either when I first started.

Flip to the back cover of my first four books and you'll see what I mean. Each short bio contains a completely different frequency. It's almost like four different music genres. No wonder success eluded me.

Frustrated, I made a firm commitment to figure it out. I knew I wouldn't be able to leave my day job until I did.

To avoid confusing my tribe, I started studying certain people I respected. I looked at their frequencies. Each successful person had credibility in one specific area.

Person	Frequency
Steve Jobs	Innovative pioneer
Dave Ramsey	Financial peacemaker
Harriet Tubman	Influential abolitionist
Marcus Buckingham	Strength-based leader
Bono	Humanitarian activist
Martin Luther King Jr.	Freedom fighter
John Eldredge	Unleashed heart

A deeper look at DJs and you see a common trait. **Their success is found in their singularity.** These men and women earned credibility because they broadcasted one frequency.

You can too.

Write Your Manifesto

The easiest way to broadcast your frequency is by writing a manifesto—a short declaration of your intent. Manifestos are sometimes political, artistic, or poetic in nature. Throughout history manifestos have changed the world for the better or for the worse. Several popular ones include Benjamin Franklin's "Thirteen Virtues," the *Humanist Manifesto*, the *Communist Manifesto*, and in recent days, the *Holstee Manifesto*.

Manifestos force readers to pick a side by communicating values and invoking action. Three quick examples prove this point.

Manifesto	Author	Action
The Sermon on the Mount	Jesus	Called followers to live out a new ethic here on earth based on principles of the heavenly kingdom.
The 95 Theses	Martin Luther	Protested common injustices within the Catholic Church and became the catalyst for the Protestant Reformation.
The Declaration of Independence	Thomas Jefferson and the Continental Congress of 1776	The thirteen American colonies declared themselves as independent states and no longer part of the British Empire.

Manifestos are definitely on the rise:

The Washington Post recently published an article titled "How the Holstee Manifesto became the new 'Just Do It.'"[1] (In less than two years over fifty million people read the manifesto.)

Life Hack added to the conversation with their own article titled "10 Insanely Awesome Inspirational Manifestos."[2] (Ten great examples, ten different styles.)

The Writer's Manifesto inspired thousands to write their own manifestos. Written by Jeff Goins, this manifesto inspired me to join the club. (Thanks, Jeff.)

I encourage you to write your own manifesto. Doing so will strengthen your community, clarity, and credibility. Here's why:

Community—Manifestos invoke a response and invite people into your tribe.

Clarity—Manifestos implant a powerful idea because they're bold and concise.

Credibility—Manifestos inject a singular frequency into your broadcast.

Manifestos are longer than a blog post, but shorter than a book. Think five hundred to five thousand words. Picking your topic is easier than you think. Just reference the first three steps in The Dream Jobber Plan. Review how you designed your story, your space, and your service. Here's why:

Story—Manifestos tell others your perspective through the backdrop of your GPS.

Space—Manifestos reflect the values you want others to experience.

Service—Manifestos not only point out a problem, they also offer a solution.

After you complete your manifesto, increase your influence, impact, and income by uploading it to Kindle Direct Publishing. When you do, you'll receive an "Author Central" website where you can share the most up-to-date information about yourself and your work with millions of readers. You'll also get the opportunity to add your biography, photos, blog, video, and tour events to your page. All these services are free.[3]

Don't skip out. Taking these steps will help you create your platform, your product, and your promotion. Here's why:

Platform—Manifestos enable you to be seen and heard.

Product—Manifestos increase your influence, impact, and income.

Promotion—Manifestos fast-track you on The Promotion Path.

Write your manifesto in any word processor and simply convert it to a PDF. Or if you prefer, create it using Keynote slides (Mac's version of PowerPoint). Then export it as a PDF. Or finally, utilize a program like Calibre, a free e-book conversion tool (www.calibre-ebook.com).

When you upload your manifesto, list it for a small price ($.99–$2.99). Consider following Brandon Clements's lead by enrolling in KDP Select. Give it away for a few days at no charge. Before you do, announce it on www.authormarketingclub.com. Add more firepower by weaving your manifesto release into a few guest posts on strategic blogs. Here's how:

Pitch the Guest Post—Check out "How to Pitch a Guest Post (Email Template Included)" by David Masters (http://bit.ly/pitchguestpost).

Write the Guest Post—See "Seven Steps to Writing a Successful Guest Post" by Jeff Goins (http://bit.ly/guestblogposts).

Create some hype before you release your manifesto to the world. Then after your KDP select campaign, give it as a free gift to those who enter their email addresses and subscribe to your blog. Your email service provider will deliver this automatically with an autoresponder. Just enter the url and away you go.

Increase your email subscriber rate by over 500 percent with LightBox software. (Find this tool as well as dozens of others at DayJob ToDreamJob.com/tools.)

Read a Manifesto

Rather then just *tell* you about manifestos, I'll *show* you mine.

Visually speaking, I prefer the online version. I created it using Keynote slides, which enable links and images. I also embedded social media features to help spread the manifesto more easily. Feel free to "borrow" my format.[4]

The Igniting Souls Manifesto
Stop Sabotaging Your Own Success
by: Kary Oberbrunner

THE END
I Sabotage My Own Success

Someone planted three questions deep inside you . . .

Who am I?
    Why am I here?
        Where am I going?

                Like a splinter in your mind,
                you've been searching for these answers
                your entire life.

And so have I.

Homesick for a place you've never been.
You want to know:

Your identity.
    Your purpose.
        Your context.

And so do I.

                On the playground of life.
                Without request, permission, or regard.
                Kids gave their opinions on the matter.

And it hurt.

Truth be told.
    These names still hurt.
        Even today.

Time to stop the hurt and start the healing.
Time to stop sabotaging your success.

This manifesto is a key for those who feel caged from their own potential.

Time to get unlocked and unstuck.
Time for the world to feel your fire as you find your voice.

If this echoes in your awareness, read on.

PART 1
My Identity
I Know Who I Am

You'll never outperform your own self-image.
If you view yourself a 2.
The world won't raise your value to a 10.

The true misfits who made their mark knew two truths.

They knew *who* they were.
And they knew *whose* they were.

You seem to forget.

And so do I.

Time to stop taking inventory on all your *shortcomings*
and *self-limiting* beliefs.

Time to start *listening* to the melody line *whispered*
in *modern* movies and *ancient* literature.

"You're more than what you've become."

Stop playing **not to lose.**
Start playing **to win.**

"Remember who you are."

Stop running from your past.

Start running toward your present.

"You once were lost, but now you're found."

Time to make your way back home.

Who am I?
Identity

PART 2
My Purpose
I Know Why I Am Here

Don't accept "their" *plans* for your *life*.
Create your own *life plan*.

If you've lost *your way*, it's because you've lost *your why*.

Stop numbing the pain.
And start embracing it.

You're in a war.
Run to the fight
Stop **running from** it.

Courage will find you in your *moment*
and never a *second* before.

Pursue the passion that haunts you in your quiet moments.
Because you've been **called** and **chosen**.

Your purpose haunts you for a reason.
For one much **BIGGER** than yourself.

Failure and *doubt* aren't your enemies.
Apathy and regret are.

They visit plenty of *people*,
Sitting on back *porches*,
Sipping glasses of **lemonade**,
Mixed with **remorse**.

Left to wonder . . .

What could be?
Should be?
and might have been?

Opportunity still *calls* their name,
But they're too *calloused* to hear.

They stopped living long before they're DEAD.

Pick a fight.

Fear reminds you you're ALIVE.

**Why am
I here?**
Purpose

PART 3
My Context
I Know Where I Should Invest My Life

Many people leave . . . to go find **themselves**.
Unfortunately . . . they have to take **themselves** along on the trip.

Running away is deceptive.

It *overpromises*
and *underdelivers*.

True travel is *discovery—not escape.*
Circumstances only change—when you do.

Freedom isn't found in a place **you go.**
But in the person **you become.**

Exchange: Captivity for *Creativity.*
Trade: Routine for *Risk.*

Take inventory of **what you'll gain.**
Stop fixating on **what you'll lose.**

Safe and Sound . . . make horrible epitaphs.

Redeem the Day
Don't simply **seize** it.
Invest your *life* in something that will *outlive* you.

Author your OPUS and make today your **masterpiece.**

THE BEGINNING
I Am a Soul on Fire

This manifesto isn't the **final** word.
It may just be the **first.**

All great conversations happen with dialogue.

We're waiting to hear **your voice.**
We're waiting to feel **your fire.**
Stop sabotaging **your success.**

Become a **Soul on Fire.**

The most powerful weapon on earth is the human **Soul on Fire.**

End with a Clear Call to Action

Conclude your manifesto with a clear action step. Why challenge people without providing a context to further the conversation? Your manifesto isn't the end, it's simply the beginning.

I conclude my manifesto by asking readers to join my tribe. If my frequency resonates with them, I want to stay connected. I want to continue serving and adding value. I'm hoping for a long-term relationship, not just a short-term read.

To see how I utilized links within my manifesto, visit my free online version. To see the text version, simply keep reading.

JOIN THIS TRIBE

To find out more about Igniting Souls and how you can get involved in our community, copy and paste this address in your browser: DayJobToDreamJob.com.

SHARE THIS MANIFESTO

You are welcome to share this manifesto with anyone and everyone. I only ask that you do not sell or change it in any way. Here are some ways to share:

Twitter | Facebook | Comments

For more ideas on how to share this manifesto and to offer feedback, visit The Igniting Souls Manifesto page.

EXPLORE THIS CONTENT

Who am I?	Why am I here?	Where am I going?
Identity	Purpose	Context
Your Secret Name	The Deeper Path	Day Job to Dream Job

Consider Adding Even More Value

Before signing off, consider providing additional content relevant to your topic. The goal is to give away your best stuff.

Recently, I created an exclusive training piece with some of my most helpful content. It's called Discover Your Purpose. This free training shows you how to:

- Know if you are living your life's true purpose.
- Understand the true cost of living a passionless life.
- Create a purpose statement for your life.
- Develop a GPS for your dreams.

Hundreds of readers chose to engage with the training. The comments we received assured us our efforts were worth it. Feel free to learn from our example (http://bit.ly/DPpurpose).

At the very end of the free training, I explain more about The Deeper Path Coaching Cohort. Whether readers join a cohort or not is irrelevant. I can rest knowing I didn't just talk about Igniting Souls. Instead, I also provided tools for the tribe to become Souls on Fire.

And at the end of the day, this is how I measure success—Igniting Souls.

Ready for the Payoff?

Now that you've experienced The Dream Jobber Plan, it's time to taste the payoff. Andy didn't just *imagine* an amazing plan to escape Shawshank. He also *implemented* the plan.

Pulling the trigger is the moment of truth.

So relax and take a deep breath.

You've prepared. And because you've prepared for the moment, the moment is prepared for you—including your escape.

Key Points

(If you RT, use #DJtoDJ to join the conversation with other DJs)

1. Success is interesting. The more you chase it, the faster it flees from you.

2. Success isn't something you achieve. It's someone you become.

3. Success begins and ends with credibility.

4. Conflicting "frequencies" create confusion. Worse than that, they also erode credibility.

5. Remember, you are your business. People don't buy *from* you. They buy *you*.

6. When you use social media to communicate mixed frequencies, you confuse people. And when you confuse them you lose them.

7. Frequencies are the intentional and unintentional attitudes, behaviors, and messages you broadcast to the world around you.

8. Success is found in singularity. People who earn credibility broadcast one frequency.

9. The easiest way to broadcast your frequency is by writing a manifesto—a short declaration of your intent.

10. Manifestos force readers to pick a side by communicating values and invoking action.

11. Manifestos not only point out a problem, they also offer a solution.

12. Manifestos implant a powerful idea because they're bold and concise.

13. Manifestos enable you to be seen and heard.

14. Your manifesto isn't the end, it's simply the beginning.

15. Because you've prepared for the moment, the moment is prepared for you.

THE PAYOFF

Zihuatanejo

A Place with No Memory

Hope is a good thing, maybe the best of things, and no good thing ever dies.

Red (Morgan Freeman)

Staring straight into your dreams, it's easy to convince yourself that captivity isn't so bad after all. Why trade what you know for what you don't? And why assume unnecessary risks? Many people never leave their day jobs for reasons such as these.

Besides, don't be surprised if you feel a little torn about leaving your day job. It's quite normal. Dan Ariely, author of *Predictably Irrational*, explains why: "Closing a door on an option is experienced as a loss, and people are willing to pay a price to avoid the emotion of a loss."[1]

When I left my day job of more than eleven years (nearly one-third of my life at the time), I left much more than a paycheck. I gave up many important things such as:

Friendships
Safety
Titles
Routine
Familiarity
Control

Predictability
Resources

Feeling a sense of loss just means you made an impact—that you mattered and others mattered to you—that you loved people and other people loved you. Cherish those relationships and memories.

Your day job was probably a good thing. It's just no longer the best thing. It reflected the person you were, not the person you are or the one you're becoming.

Your day job served a purpose and hopefully you served it—with integrity. But to advance, you must let go.

When Is the Right Time to Leave Your Day Job?

Months before I left my day job, I remember chatting with one of my mentors, John Maxwell. I asked him how to know if it's the right time to leave your day job.[2] From our conversation, I drew the following conclusions:

The Right Time to Leave—A Good Type of Restlessness

1. When you've fulfilled your calling.
2. When you're being pulled toward improvement.
3. When you're embracing a new assignment.
4. When you've reached your potential.
5. When you've learned as much as you can from the people around you.

The Wrong Time to Leave—A Bad Type of Restlessness

1. When you're bored.
2. When you're running from improvement.
3. When you're escaping your current assignment.
4. When you haven't paid the price.
5. When you think you're better than the people around you.

John concluded his thoughts that day by saying something that ripped right through me. He said, "Remember, don't move anywhere else until you've done the best where you are."

Ouch!

Because I had done my best at my day job, I realized my departure was inevitable. Even though I knew this, my organization didn't. Preparing to make this announcement felt incredibly difficult.

Because I had a visible role within my day job, I needed to communicate my departure to all one thousand members at once.

You can imagine the fear I felt. Forget slipping out the back door! I had to announce my escape from a stage—literally. During the week of my announcement many thoughts went through my head. When I thought about disappointing people, I felt panic. Yet when I thought about pleasing God, I felt peace.

The day of the announcement went better than expected. My wife, Kelly, stood by my side in support. To our surprise, at the conclusion of the news, the entire organization cheered and gave us a standing ovation.

Funny, huh? The only standing ovation I ever received in my life came the moment I announced I was leaving. But all joking aside, their genuine appreciation strengthened my confidence in a very emotional moment.

Your Plan Leads to Zihuatanejo

Andy eventually escaped Shawshank Prison. By developing his plan *and* envisioning his payoff, he ran toward his future and escaped his present.

Obviously he didn't want Shawshank—no one would. But toward the end of the movie we find out what he actually wanted—a life in Zihuatanejo.

Andy told his friend Red about this little Mexican town right on the Pacific. He chose the Pacific because the Mexicans say the ocean has no memory. Plagued with a heavy past, Andy wanted to create a new life. He informed Red about his dream to open a little hotel right on the beach. He'd buy a worthless old boat and fix it up like new to take guests out charter fishing.

Unable to formulate his own dream, Red was invited by Andy into his. Able to see beyond their current captivity, Andy painted a picture that played to Red's strengths. "You know, a place like that, I'd need a man who can get things."[3]

Institutionalized by now, Red simply shrugged off the dream. He couldn't imagine life beyond bars.

Thankfully Andy did. His plan enabled him to dream bigger. DJs are funny like that. They inspire the rest of us. They force us to face our own fear. Their action demands us to make our own decision.

Red responded to Andy's courage by finding his own. *The Shawshank Redemption* concludes much like this book. Red escaped his day job, broke parole, and boarded a bus to find Andy in Zihuatanejo. On his way to pursuing his own dream job he sat on the bus and reflected:

> I find I am so excited I can barely sit still or hold a thought in my head.
> I think it is the excitement only a free man can feel, a free man at the
> start of a long journey whose conclusion is uncertain.[4]

In a way, your conclusion is uncertain too. It rests squarely upon your shoulders.

So let me make it simple. Like Red, you really only have one of two choices.

Get busy living or get busy dying.

Which one is it?

Appendix A

Two Quick but Critical Reflections

Reflection 1—Your Partnerships Matter

Before I even prayed, David Brandershorst was an answer to my prayers.

Because he was a true friend, Red played a significant role in Andy's escape from Shawshank. Because David is a true friend, he played a significant role in my escape from my day job.

In the early days, when my dream was still a part-time passion, David came along and supported me. When *Your Secret Name* launched, David volunteered and helped me spread the message of hope and healing. Support came first via encouragement and then evolved along the way. Eventually he created resources, managed technology, and taught content.

We ran our first Your Secret Name conference in early 2011. Our products and services expanded significantly with each year. David transitioned from occasional volunteer to full-time partner.

Although there's much more to the story, I included this much in this book because I want to prepare you for your own partnerships. Healthy ones propel your business. Unhealthy ones kill it. One of

my friends, Paul Martinelli, says, "Partnerships begin on the back
of a napkin at a party and end in front of a judge in a courtroom."
Translation? Tread slowly, as in all relationships.

Don't simply accept help; prequalify your partnerships. They'll
keep you (and your partnerships) from trouble. Keep three filters in
the forefront of your mind—strategy, intentionality, and clarity.

Strategy—Know the Rank

1. PARTNER UP

Partnering up takes place when two individuals or organizations
form a longer-term, mutually beneficial relationship. True *partnering
up* occurs when each party brings unique and specific value to the
relationship in an area where the other is lacking.

2. COLLABORATE ACROSS

Collaborating across takes place when two individuals or organizations form a shorter-term, event-based relationship. True *collaborating
across* occurs when each party brings similar value to the relationship.

3. MENTOR AROUND

Mentoring around takes place when two individuals form a flexible, intentional relationship. True *mentoring around* occurs when
one party clearly brings more value to the relationship and shares
their experiences, usually as responses to the other party's questions.

Intentionality—Know the Rationale

Because of your success, people will come to you and propose
partnerships, if they haven't already. But a request alone isn't a good
enough reason to partner. They need to know enough about you
and your business to explain why the partnership will be beneficial
to both of you. Put responsibility back on them, since they're the
ones proposing.

People will tell you, "We should partner together." Your reply
should be, "Sounds interesting. Why do you think so?" If they can't
explain their rationale, then they don't have enough awareness about
their value or *your* business. Chances are they like you and they're

attracted to you. Acknowledge the honor in their requests, but treat them as potential clients, not as permanent partners.

Clarity—Know the Roles

David and I use a *what, why, where* model to keep it simple. We each know what we do, why we do it, and where we fit in. It creates efficiencies and prevents us from tripping over each other. This simple exercise took us three hours because of the relevant issues it naturally raised. I encourage you to try it in the future with your teams.

1. WHAT DO I DO?

Kary—I'm a soul on fire igniting souls on fire.

David—I'm transforming and helping others transform.

2. WHY DO I DO IT?

Kary—Because souls aren't on fire, and we don't see things the way they are but the way we are.

David—Because people need to reach their potential by becoming all God created them to be.

3. WHERE DO I FIT IN?

Kary—I create a process that ignites souls on fire through speaking, writing, and coaching.

David—I create structures and deliver resources that fuel transformation.

Reflection 2—Your Legacy Matters

"I'm lucky I discovered my dream job," Molly the librarian told me.

I believed her. Who wouldn't? Her enthusiasm for kids radiated in her words and actions. I met her at the summer reading table. My kids had completed all their "bases" and earned free tickets to the minor league baseball game in our city.

"Congratulations, kids!" she exclaimed. "I bet you enjoyed reading your books this summer."

In the first thirty seconds of watching her interact with my kids, I could tell Molly had discovered her dream job. Curious about DJs of all kinds—librarians included—I asked her the quick backstory for her discovery.

She gave all the credit to her parents. "They absolutely loved their jobs and communicated their excitement regularly to us kids," she told me. "My mom worked as a speech pathologist in the public school system and my dad as a district attorney. Seeing them on fire, I couldn't imagine doing anything but what I absolutely love too."

Because her parents found passion to pursue their dream jobs, Molly found the courage to pursue hers too.

If you're stuck in a day job, don't forget Carl Jung's words: "The greatest burden a child must bear is the unlived life of the parent."[1]

Remember—you wound your legacy by staying in a job that's killing you. And the opposite is true too. You give kids permission to pursue their dream jobs when you pursue yours.

Appendix B

Four Types of Prisoners

Overcome disengagement and despair.
Craft your Dream Jobber Plan.
Discover creativity and hope.

Day Job + No Dream Jobber Plan = DISENGAGED	Day Job + Dream Jobber Plan = CREATIVE
No Day Job + No Dream Jobber Plan = DESPAIRING	No Day Job + Dream Jobber Plan = HOPEFUL

Appendix C

Dream Job Bootcamp

Congratulations! You've invested in yourself and your dream by reading this book. Your legacy is worth it.

Our website will give you plenty of additional tools to plan your escape. Make sure to join our growing tribe of DJs from around the world (DayJobToDreamJob.com). We'll save you a spot. It's a great way to stay connected, challenged, and encouraged.

If you'd like additional help planning to escape your day job and launch your dream job—I'M IN.

We have an experience that's perfect for you and your situation. We call it Dream Job Bootcamp.

The purpose is simple—*jailbreak your job and turn your passion into your full-time gig.* Dream Job Bootcamp helps you customize your Dream Jobber Plan and prepare you and your plan for implementation.

Our Dream Job Bootcamps range from an online course to an in-person experience at "Shawshank Prison," the Ohio State Reformatory.

This one-of-kind experience allows you to process your own situation by seeing how Andy escaped his, literally. I serve as your transformational tour guide and I spend time personally coaching each attendee. Together, we'll craft your Day Jobber Plan at the award-winning *sparkspace* (featured in Step Two—Design Your Space). Prepare for a life-changing experience.

If you're interested in taking your next step, we have a Dream Job Bootcamp perfect for you and your budget. Come check us out: DayJobToDreamJob.com.

> The tragedy of life is not that it ends so soon,
> but that we wait so long to begin it.
> W. M. Lewis

DREAM JOB
BOOTCAMP™

Acknowledgments

To My Dream Team

THE FANS

Desiree Arney, Kim Maxwell, Kim Gowdy, Laura Prisc, Ruby Muza
Cooley, Barry Smith, Louise Elliott, Tracy Worley, Billy Harris,
Jon Giganti, Frances Capoccia, Benjamin Hampton,
John Toth, Lisa Shearman
And the rest. You know who you are.

THE FREELANCERS

Mike Rohde

THE FRIENDS

Truth Tellers
Kelly Oberbrunner, David Branderhorst,
Chet Scott, Paul Martinelli

Edifiers
Keegan, Isabel, Addison, Mike Oberbrunner, Linda Oberbrunner, Sarah Oberbrunner, Mike Myers, Emily Myers, Mike Hoppe, June Hoppe, Bob Hosack, Ruth Anderson, Elizabeth Kool

Challengers
Scott Fay, The Deeper Path Team, Your Secret Name Team, John Maxwell

THE FUNDERS

Time Investors
Carol Kuck

Talent Investors
Kelly Stults, Ron Kuck, Chaz Freutel

Notes

Citizens of Shawshank

1. Right Management ManPower Group, "Survey Finds Continued Worker Discontent," November 27, 2012, http://www.right.com/news-and-events/press-releases/2012-press-releases/item24318.aspx.

2. Ibid.

Do You Feel Trapped?

1. Dean Schabner, "Americans Work More Than Anyone," *ABC News*, May 1, 2013, http://abcnews.go.com/US/story?id=93364&page=1#.UcRPUJUijFJ.

2. Ibid.

3. "Great Recession," *Wikipedia*, http://en.wikipedia.org/wiki/Great_Recession, accessed June 25, 2013.

4. L. P. Jacks, *Education through Recreation* (New York: Harper & Brothers, 1932), 1.

Do You Feel Enslaved?

1. "Passive Income," *The Free Dictionary by Farlex*, http://financial-dictionary.thefreedictionary.com/passive+income, accessed June 25, 2013.

2. *Your Secret Name*, http://www.yoursecretname.com.

3. "Your Secret Name," YouTube video, 4:15, posted by Kary Oberbrunner on March 2, 2010, https://www.youtube.com/watch?v=7-xavMhcZK8&feature=player_embedded.

4. To read their stories, visit "Secret Stories," *Your Secret Name*, http://www.yoursecretname.com/category/secret-stories/.

5. See more information on team members Gill Scott at http://www.linkedin.com/in/gillscottmotiveleadership and Elias Kanaris at http://www.eliaskanaris.com.

6. See more information on Patrick Nsereko and Autumn Neighbors at *Your Secret Name Team*, http://www.yoursecretname.com/team/.

7. Seth Godin, "Fearlessness is not the same as the absence of fear," *Seth's Blog*, June 23, 2013, http://sethgodin.typepad.com/seths_blog/2013/06/fearlessness-is-not-the-same-as-the-absence-of-fear.html.

8. Joseph Campbell, *The Power of Myth* (New York: Anchor, 1991), 4.

Do You Feel Dissatisfied?

1. Tim Ferriss, *The 4-Hour Workweek* (New York: Harmony, 2009), 75.

2. "Billionaires' Advice for New College Grads," *Forbes*, http://www.forbes.com/pictures/edek45fghe/steve-jobs-live-each-day-as-if-it-was-your-last/, accessed June 27, 2013.

Why The "When" Is "Now"

1. Darren Hardy, "The Vault is Open," June 4, 2013, http://darrenhardy.success.com/2013/06/the-vault-door-is-open/.

2. Ibid.

3. Triin Linamagi, "10 Mind-Blowing Facts About Mobile Users," *TextMagic Blog*, June 12, 2013, http://www.textmagic.com/blog/10-mind-blowing-facts-about-mobile-users/.

4. Several websites devoted to contacting celebrities are http://www.wikihow.com/Contact-Famous-Celebrities, http://www.thehandbook.com/celebrities, and http://www.celebrityendorsement.com.

5. Sam Costello, "How Many Apps Are in the iPhone App Store," *About.com*, http://ipod.about.com/od/iphonesoftwareterms/qt/apps-in-app-store.htm, accessed June 28, 2013.

6. For more information on many different apps, I suggest Matt Hamilton, "25 Unusual and Inspiring Uses for Your iPhone," *AppStorm,* April 8, 2010, http://iphone.appstorm.net/roundups/25-unusual-and-inspiring-uses-for-your-iphone/; and Peter May, "10 Off-the-wall iPhone Apps," *How Stuff Works*, http://www.howstuffworks.com/cell-phone-apps/10-off-the-wall-iphone-apps.htm/printable, accessed June 29, 2013.

7. "Elven Gifts from Lothlorien," *Wikia*, http://lotr.wikia.com/wiki/Elven_Gifts_from_Lothlorien, accessed June 29, 2013.

8. "John le Carré > Quotes > Quotable Quote," *Good Reads*, http://www.goodreads.com/quotes/125728-a-desk-is-a-dangerous-place-from-which-to-view, accessed January 26, 2014.

9. Michael Myers, Talents Tutoring Service, http://www.magnifyingtalents.com, accessed June 29, 2013.

10. United States Department of Labor, "Bureau of Labor Statistics—Labor Force Statistics from the Current Population Survey," http://data.bls.gov/timeseries/LNS14000000, accessed April 22, 2013.

11. United States Department of Labor, "News Release—Number of jobs held, labor market activity, and earnings growth among the youngest baby boomers: results from a longitudinal survey," July 25, 2012, http://www.bls.gov/news.release/pdf/nlsoy.pdf.

12. Carl Bialik, "Seven Careers in a Lifetime? Think Twice, Researchers Say," *The Wall Street Journal*, September 4, 2010, http://online.wsj.com/article/SB10001424052748704206804575468162805877990.html.

13. United States Department of Labor, "Bureau of Labor Statistics—Employee Tenure Summary," September 18, 2012, http://www.bls.gov/news.release/tenure.nr0.htm.

14. Dan Miller, *48 Days to the Work You Love*, (Nashville: B & H Publishing Group, 2010), http://www.amazon.com/Days-Work-You-Love-Preparing/dp/1433669331.

15. The Deeper Path Cohort; visit http://www.deeperpathbook.com/cohort/.

16. The engagement levels in China, Singapore, and Germany are much worse than the United States. See http://businessjournal.gallup.com/content/117376/employee-dis engagement-plagues-germany.aspx; http://businessjournal.gallup.com/content/22720/worker-disengagement-continues-cost-singapore.aspx; and http://businessjournal.gallup.com/content/160406/china-workplace-problem.aspx.

17. Kelli Grant, "Americans hate their jobs and even perks don't help," *Today CNBC*, June 24, 2013, http://www.today.com/money/americans-hate-their-jobs-even-perks-dont-help-6C10423977.

18. Ibid.

19. Jerry Ruhl, "Lecture: The Unlived Life," *Oregon Friends of C.G. Jung*, http://ofj.org/lecture/lecture-unlived-life, accessed January 26, 2014.

20. "High School Dropout Statistics," *Statistic Brain*, http://www.statisticbrain.com/high-school-dropout-statistics/, accessed June 30, 2013.

21. Miller, *48 Days to the Work You Love*, 22.

22. Jon Jeter, "Slavery 2010," *The Root*, February 10, 2010, http://www.theroot.com/articles/politics/2010/02/black_history_month_are_we_still_slaves.html.

23. "The Shawshank Redemption," *IMDb*, http://www.imdb.com/title/tt0111161/trivia, accessed July 1, 2013.

24. "AFI's 100 Years . . . 100 Movies," *Wikipedia*, http://en.wikipedia.org/wiki/AFI%27s_100_Years...100_Movies, accessed July 1, 2013.

25. "The Shawshank Redemption," *Total Film*, November 8, 2006, http://www.totalfilm.com/features/the-shawshank-redemption.

26. "IMDb Charts: IMDb Top 250," *IMDb*, http://www.imdb.com/chart/top, accessed July 1, 2013.

27. Roger Ebert, "The Shawshank Redemption," September 23, 1994, http://www.rogerebert.com/reviews/the-shawshank-redemption-1994.

28. Frank Darabont, "The Shawshank Redemption," *IMSDb*, http://www.imsdb.com/scripts/Shawshank-Redemption,-The.html, accessed July 2, 2013.

29. Ibid.

30. Ibid.

31. Ibid.

Step One: DESIGN Your Story

1. For example, see UNCO Industries, "Starting Your Own Worm Farming Business," http://www.vermiculture.com/starting_a_business.html, accessed July 2, 2013.

2. "About Worms," http://www.worms4earth.com/aboutworms.php, accessed July 2, 2013.

3. Berta Delgado, "Fruit of His Labors," *The Dallas Morning News*, January 4, 2003, repr. "Howard G. Hendricks," *Dallas Theological Seminary*, http://www.dts.edu/about/profiles/Howard_G_Hendricks, accessed July 2, 2013.

4. "The Matrix," *IMDb*, http://www.imdb.com/title/tt0133093/quotes, accessed January 26, 2014.

5. "Maya Angelou," Women Who Changed America, http://www.womenwho changedamerica.org/profile/maya-angelou, accessed January 26, 2014.

6. Charles R. Cross, *Heavier Than Heaven* (New York: Hyperion, 2002), 351–52.

7. "Kurt Cobain," *Wikipedia*, http://en.wikipedia.org/wiki/Kurt_Cobain, accessed July 3, 2013.

8. "Cobain's Suicide Note," *DateJesus.com*, http://www.datejesus.com/sermons/cobain/suicide.html, accessed July 3, 2013.

9. Ivan Klíma, *Love and Garbage* (New York: Knopf, 1991), 117.

10. "Guru," *Merriam-Webster*, http://www.merriam-webster.com/dictionary/guru, accessed July 5, 2013.

11. "Never, Ever Give Up. Arthur's Inspirational Transformation!," YouTube video, 4:55, posted by Diamond Dallas on April 30, 2012, http://www.youtube.com/watch?v=qX9FSZJu448.

12. Malcolm Gladwell, "The Tipping Point," Gladwell.com, http://gladwell.com/the-tipping-point/, accessed July 6, 2013.

13. "About Dave," DaveRamsey.com, http://www.daveramsey.com/company/about-dave/, accessed July 6, 2013.

14. "Dave Ramsey," *Wikipedia*, http://en.wikipedia.org/wiki/Dave_Ramsey, accessed July 7, 2013.

15. "About Dr. Sacks," Oliver Sacks, M.D., http://www.oliversacks.com/about-the-author/about-dr-sacks/, accessed July 7, 2013.

16. Katie Moisse, Bob Woodruff, James Hill, and Lana Zak, "Gabby Giffords: Finding Voice through Music Therapy," *ABC News*, November 14, 2011, http://abc news.go.com/Health/w_MindBodyNews/gabby-giffords-finding-voice-music-therapy/story?id=14903987.

17. Kurt Badenhausen, "How Michael Jordan Still Earns $80 Million a Year," *Forbes*, February 14, 2013, http://www.forbes.com/sites/kurtbadenhausen/2013/02/14/how-michael-jordan-still-earns-80-million-a-year/.

18. Ibid.

19. "What Is GPS?" Garmin, http://www8.garmin.com/aboutGPS/, accessed July 8, 2013.

20. Ferriss, *4-Hour Workweek*, 167.

21. The New Man Project, http://www.thenewmanproject.com, accessed July 8, 2013.

22. Guy Chmieleski "Catalyst/Andy Stanley/Be Present," *FaithOnCampus*, October 6, 2011, http://faithoncampus. com/catalyst-andy-stanley-be-present/.

23. Brendon Burchard, *The Millionaire Messenger*, (New York: Morgan James, 2011), 44.

24. Ferriss, *4-Hour Workweek*, 168.

25. Ryan Deiss, "How to Create Your First Kindle Book This Weekend," 2012, http://www.long-distance-lover.com/wp-content/uploads/2012/09/HowToCreateYour FirstKindleBookInaWeekend.pdf, accessed July 9, 2013.

26. "About Alltop," Alltop.com, http://alltop.com/about/, accessed July 10, 2013.

27. Ecclesiastes 1:9.

28. U2, "The Fly," *MP3 Lyrics*, http://www.mp3lyrics.org/u/u2/the-fly/, accessed August 4, 2013.

29. "Synthesis," *The Free Dictionary by Farlex*, http://www.thefreedictionary.com/synthesis, accessed July 10, 2013.

30. A picture of a "synthesized" book: http://bit.ly/sythesizerpic., accessed December 18, 2013.

31. "Apple Steve Jobs The Crazy Ones - NEVER BEFORE AIRED 1997," YouTube video, 1:01, posted by S Jackson on February 1, 2009, http://www.youtube.com/watch?v=8rwsuXHA7RA.

32. Napoleon Hill, "Chapter Five: Specialized Knowledge," *Think and Grow Rich* (orig. pub. Meriden, CT: Ralston Society, 1937), http://www.sacred-texts.com/nth/tgr/tgr10.htm, accessed July 10, 2013.

Step Two: DESIGN Your Space

1. I loved the food, the one time I went. Rodizio Grill, http://www.rodiziogrill.com/columbus, accessed July 12, 2013.

2. Thanks to Jon Acuff for the inspiration behind this thought.

3. "The Eureka! Ranch," http://www.eurekaranch.com/the-ranch-facility.html, accessed July 13, 2013.

4. Sparkspace, http://www.sparkspace.com/public-events/, accessed July 13, 2013.

Step Three: DESIGN Your Service

1. Eric Hoffer, *Ordeal of Change*, (Cutchogue, NY: Buccaneer Books, 1976), 171.

2. Fast Company Staff, "A Dislike for Change," January 12, 2006, http://www.fastcompany.com/930982/dislike-change.

3. Tom Peters, "The Brand Called You," *Fast Company*, http://www.fastcompany.com/28905/brand-called-you, accessed January 27, 2014.

4. Ibid.

5. Ibid.

6. Dan Schawbel, "How Recruiters Use Social Networks to Make Hiring Decisions Now," *Time*, July 9, 2012, http://business.time.com/2012/07/09/how-recruiters-use-social-networks-to-make-hiring-decisions-now/.

7. Ibid.

8. Career Builder, "Thirty-seven percent of companies use social networks to research potential job candidates, according to new CareerBuilder Survey," April 18, 2012, http://www.careerbuilder.com/share/aboutus/pressreleasesdetail.aspx?id=pr691&sd=4%2F18%2F2012&ed=4%2F18%2F2099.

9. Catharine Smith and Craig Kanalley, "Fired Over Facebook: 13 Posts That Got People CANNED," *Huffington Post*, July 26, 2010, http://www.huffingtonpost.com/2010/07/26/fired-over-facebook-posts_n_659170.html#slide=115650.

10. Catharine Smith and Bianca Bosker, "Fired Over Twitter: 13 Tweets That Got People CANNED," *Huffington Post*, July 14, 2010, http://www.huffingtonpost.com/2010/07/15/fired-over-twitter-tweets_n_645884.html#s112801title=Cisco_Fatty_Loses.

11. Thanks to Wayne Dyer for the indirect quote.

12. Viktor E. Frankl, *Man's Search for Meaning* (Boston: Beacon Press, 2006), http://books.google.com/books/about/Man_s_Search_for_Meaning.html?id=F-Q_xGjWBi8C.

13. Grant, "Americans hate their jobs and even perks don't help."

14. Miller, *48 Days to the Work You Love*, http://www.amazon.com/Days-Work-You-Love-Preparing/dp/1433669331.

15. John Maxwell, *The 21 Irrefutable Laws of Leadership* (Nashville: Thomas Nelson, 1997), 106.

16. "Luke Fickell," *Wikipedia*, http://en.wikipedia.org/wiki/Luke_Fickell, accessed July 16, 2013.

17. "Bob's Red Mill," *Wikipedia*, http://en.wikipedia.org/wiki/Bob's_Red_Mill, accessed July 16, 2013.

18. Chris Guillebeau, *The $100 Startup* (New York: Random House, 2012), 47.

19. Vishen Lakhiani, "How to Craft a Brilliant Guarantee with 'Risk Reversal' (Part 1)," *Mind Valley Insights*, www.mindvalleyinsights.com/choose-risk-reversal-guarantee-business-needs-part-1/, accessed July 17, 2013.

20. Best Buy, "Return and Exchange Policy," http://www.bestbuy.com/site/help-topics/return-exchange-policy/pcmcat260800050014.c?id=pcmcat260800050014, accessed January 28, 2014.

21. Lowe's, "Returns and Refunds Policy," http://www.lowes.com/cd_Returns+and+Refunds+Policy_33243642_, accessed July 17, 2013.

22. Zappos, "Shipping and Returns," http://www.zappos.com/shipping-and-returns, accessed July 18, 2013.

23. Peters, "Brand Called You."

Step Four: CREATE Your Platform

1. Gene Weingarten, "Pearls Before Breakfast," *Washington Post*, April 8, 2007, http://www.washingtonpost.com/wp-dyn/content/article/2007/04/04/AR2007040401721.html.

2. Ibid.

3. Ibid.

4. Michael Hyatt, "Why You Need a Platform to Succeed," http://michaelhyatt.com/platform, accessed July 18, 2013.

5. "Seth Godin," *Wikipedia*, http://en.wikipedia.org/wiki/Seth_Godin, accessed July 18, 2013.

6. Seth Godin, "Permission Marketing," *Seth's Blog*, January 31, 2008, http://sethgodin.typepad.com/seths_blog/2008/01/permission-mark.html.

7. John C. Maxwell, "Connectors Do the Difficult Work of Keeping It Simple," October 18, 2009, http://johnmaxwellonleadership.com/2009/10/18/connectors-do-the-difficult-work-of-keeping-it-simple/.

8. Thanks to Chris Brogan for starting my thinking in this direction. See Chris Brogan, "A Simple Presence Framework," June 15, 2009, http://www.chrisbrogan.com/a-simple-presence-framework/. I also found value in his Master Class.

9. Google also offers a more robust, paid version. See http://www.google.com/alerts.

10. "Goethe," To Inspire, http://www.toinspire.com/author.asp?author=Goethe, accessed January 28, 2014.

11. George Anders, *The Rare Find* (New York: Portfolio, 2012), 119–20.

12. *Inception*, directed by Christopher Nolan (Warner Bros., 2010), DVD.

13. Seth Godin, *Tribes: We Need You to Lead Us* (New York: Portfolio, 2008), http://www.amazon.com/Tribes-We-Need-You-Lead/dp/1591842336, accessed January 28, 2014.

14. Michael Hyatt, "What I Learned about Leadership from a Fight with My Wife," August 18, 2011, http://michaelhyatt.com/what-i-learned-about-leadership-from-a-fight-with-my-wife.html.

15. You can access the video here: http://bit.ly/DPpurpose.

16. Hyatt, "Why You Need a Platform to Succeed."

17. Godin, "Permission Marketing."

Step Five: CREATE Your Product

1. Ann Oldenburg, "Jillian Michaels shows she once weighed 175 pounds," *USA TODAY*, June 17, 2010, http://content.usatoday.com/communities/entertainment/post/2010/06/jillian-michaels-shows-she-once-weighed-175-pounds/1#.Ue7CxhZ-MUU.

2. "Jillian Michaels Biography," *Biography*, http://www.biography.com/people/jillian-michaels-5948?page=1, accessed July 20, 2013.

3. "Jillian's Bio," *Jillian Michaels*, http://www.jillianmichaels.com/fit/about-jillian/bio, accessed July 20, 2013.

4. Todd Eliason, "John Maxwell: A Life of Leadership and Inspiration," *SUCCESS*, http://www.success.com/articles/606-a-life-of-leadership-and-inspiration, accessed July 20, 2013.

5. "Golden Gavel Award," Toastmasters International, http://www.toastmasters.org/goldengavel, accessed July 20, 2013.

6. Eliason, "John Maxwell: A Life of Leadership and Inspiration."

7. "What We Do," Equip, http://www.iequip.org, accessed July 20, 2013.

8. "Brian Moran," *The Rise to the Top*, http://www.therisetothetop.com/people/brian-moran/, accessed July 20, 2013.

9. Yaro Starak, "From College Baseball Professional, to Facebook Advertising Expert, Brian Moran Shares How He Made a Million in His First Full Time Year Online," *Entrepreneurs-Journey*, July 24, 2012, http://www.entrepreneurs-journey.com/11055/brian-moran/.

10. "Teleseminars," *Wikipedia*, http://en.wikipedia.org/wiki/Teleseminars, accessed July 20, 2013.

11. "Web Conferencing," *Wikipedia*, http://en.wikipedia.org/wiki/Web_conferencing, accessed July 20, 2013.

12. Sid Savara, "How to Start and Run a Mastermind Group," *Life Hack*, http://www.lifehack.org/articles/productivity/how-to-start-and-run-a-mastermind-group.html, accessed July 20, 2013.

13. Joel Falconer, "How to Use Parkinson's Law to Your Advantage," *Life Hack*, http://www.lifehack.org/articles/productivity/how-to-use-parkinsons-law-to-your-advantage.html, accessed July 20, 2013.

14. "Parkinson's Law in Time Management," *Process Policy*, https://processpolicy.com/parkinsons-law.htm, accessed July 20, 2013.

Step Six: CREATE Your Promotion

1. More about my friend Chet and his business Built To Lead: http://www.builttolead.com.

2. "Four Rules Every Female Entrepreneur Should Follow," *Business 2 Community*, http://www.business2community.com/leadership/four-rules-every-female-entrepreneur-follow-0635570#!tGqjS, accessed January 28, 2014.

3. You can access the video here: http://bit.ly/DPpurpose.

4. Seth Godin, "Polishing Perfect," *Seth's Blog*, June 11, 2013, http://sethgodin.typepad.com/seths_blog/2013/06/polishing-perfect.html.

5. Juliet Lapidos, "Why Did It Take Google So Long to Take Gmail Out of 'Beta?'" *Slate*, July 7, 2009, http://www.slate.com/articles/news_and_politics/recycled/2009/07/why_did_it_take_google_so_long_to_take_gmail_out_of_beta.html.

Step Seven: MAINTAIN Your Community

1. For more information about Brandon, visit http://www.brandonclements.com.

2. "What Is Kickstarter?" Kickstarter, http://www.kickstarter.com/hello?ref=nav, accessed December 18, 2013.

3. Brandon Clements, *Every Bush Is Burning*, http://everybushisburning.com, accessed July 20, 2013.

4. For more information about Jeff, visit http://goinswriter.com.

5. For more information, visit Kindle Direct Publishing at https://kdp.amazon.com/self-publishing/KDPSelect.

6. Darabont, "The Shawshank Redemption," http://www.imsdb.com/scripts/Shawshank-Redemption,-The.html.

7. Seth Godin, "Piracy? You wish," *The Domino Project*, http://www.thedominoproject.com/2012/04/piracy-you-wish.html, accessed July 21, 2013.

Step Eight: MAINTAIN Your Clarity

1. Adam McCampbell, "Adam P. McCampbell: Opus," http://bit.ly/adamopus, accessed July 21, 2013.

2. "Why VisionSpark?" VisionSpark, www.vision-spark.com, accessed July 21, 2013.

3. Built to Lead.com, http://www.builttolead.com, accessed July 22, 2013.

Step Nine: MAINTAIN Your Credibility

1. Olga Khazan, "How the Holstee manifesto became the new 'Just Do It,'" *Washington Post*, November 17, 2011, http://www.washingtonpost.com/business/on-small-business/how-the-holstee-manifesto-became-the-new-just-do-it/2011/11/17/gIQA2AYyUN_story.html.

2. Mike Vardy, "10 Insanely Awesome Inspirational Manifestos," *Life Hack*, http://www.lifehack.org/articles/lifestyle/10-awesome-inspirational-manifestos.html, accessed July 24, 2013.

3. For more on Kindle Direct Publishing, visit https://kdp.amazon.com. For more on Amazon Author Central, visit "All About Amazon Author Central," www.authorcentral.amazon.com, and "Amazon Author Central," http://bit.ly/authorcent.

4. Get your free copy of my manifesto at DayJobToDreamJob.com.

Zihuatanejo

1. John Tierney, "The Advantages of Closing a Few Doors," *New York Times*, February 26, 2008, http://www.nytimes.com/2008/02/26/science/26tier.html?page wanted=all&_r=0.

2. Another helpful resource is Ron Edmondson, "When Is It Time to Quit? 10 Scenarios to Help Decide," *Church Leaders*, http://www.churchleaders.com/pastors/pastor-articles/168300-ron-edmondson-it-time-to-quit-10-scenarios-to-help-decide.html, accessed July 25, 2013.

3. Darabont, "The Shawshank Redemption," http://www.imsdb.com/scripts/Shawshank-Redemption,-The.html.

4. Ibid.

Appendix A

1. Ruhl, "Lecture: The Unlived Life," http://ofj.org/lecture/lecture-unlived-life.

Kary Oberbrunner left his day job to pursue his dream job—igniting souls. Through his writing, speaking, and coaching, he helps individuals and organizations clarify who they are, why they are here, and where they should invest their time and energy.

Kary struggled to find his own distinct voice and passion. As a young man, he suffered from severe stuttering, depression, and self-injury. Today a transformed man, Kary invests his time helping others achieve their true potential. He is the founder of Redeem the Day, which serves the business community, and Igniting Souls, which serves the nonprofit community.

The author of several books, he has earned his doctorate in Transformational Leadership. Kary also serves as a founding partner on the John Maxwell Team. He and his wife, Kelly, are blessed with three amazing children.

Connect at: KaryOberbrunner.com

DREAM JOB BOOTCAMP™

THE PURPOSE IS SIMPLE:
Jailbreak your job and turn your passion into your full-time gig.

Dream Job Bootcamp helps you customize your Dream Jobber Plan and prepare you and your plan for implementation.

Let us help you make your dreams a reality.

Our Dream Job Bootcamps range from an online edition to an in-person bootcamp at Shawshank.

If you're interested in taking your next step, we have a Dream Job Bootcamp perfect for you and your budget.

Visit
DAYJOBTODREAMJOB.COM

Also from
KARY OBERBRUNNER

THE DEEPER PATH

Five Steps That Let Your Hurts Lead to Your Healing

"If you want to make your life a masterpiece, then read *The Deeper Path*."
—MARK SANBORN, *New York Times, Wall Street Journal,* and *BusinessWeek* bestselling author of *The Fred Factor*

KARY OBERBRUNNER

TAKE YOUR NEXT STEP
Join a Deeper Path Coaching Cohort

Imagine author Kary Oberbrunner leading you through a transformational process where you journey through your Pain and into your potential.

Imagine finding clarity by authoring your OPUS and strengthening your CORE.

Hundreds of people have found freedom and purpose through this powerful experience. Participants can join from anywhere in the world.

Find out more at
DEEPERPATHBOOK.COM

What's the cost of not living in light of your TRUE POTENTIAL?